TWAYNE'S UNITED STATES AUTHORS SERIES

Sylvia E. Bowman, *Editor*

INDIANA UNIVERSITY

W. H. Auden

W. H. Auden

by GEORGE T. WRIGHT

University of Minnesota

Twayne Publishers, Inc.   : :   New York

To my mother
and the memory of my father

Preface

W. H. AUDEN'S place among modern poets has long been uncertain. The main reason is not that his work is uneven (most poets are uneven), but that its variety has obscured its unity, and we do not see how we should read him. Some of his best qualities put us off; we are suspicious of his elegance, his diversity, his wit. Most of all, his tone is puzzling; we often do not know how to separate parody from wisdom, or mockery from sympathy.

In spite of his voluminous writing about his art, only very recently have we come to see his career as coherent and consistent. The two books that have contributed most to this insight are Monroe Spears' *The Poetry of W. H. Auden: The Disenchanted Island* (1963) and John G. Blair's *The Poetic Art of W. H. Auden* (1965). Spears' work is an indispensable handbook for students and scholars, for it provides helpful background materials on all aspects of Auden's career. But, although it underlines certain continuing concerns of Auden, it is only partly successful in showing the unity of Auden's work. Blair's book, emphasizing Auden's enduring hostility to Romanticism and his continuing search for allegorical poetic techniques, is the first extended criticism that sees his work as the coherent whole that it more or less is. But Blair's approach is analytical rather than historical.

My first objective, therefore, in this study of Auden is to make more intelligible the bewildering changes in thought, style, and feeling that mark Auden's poetry. The oddness of his collections (especially the 1945 *Collected Poetry* and the 1950 *Collected Shorter Poems*), which the late Joseph Warren Beach analyzed in *The Making of the Auden Canon* (1957), has contributed to this bewilderment, partly because of Auden's extensive and sometimes confusing revisions and omissions of earlier poems, but principally because of the arrangement of the poems in alphabetical order by first lines instead of chronologically. This arrangement, by obscuring Auden's development, implies that each poem should be valued for its individual artistry, not for establishing some point about the history of the poet's mind.

Nevertheless, to look at the poems historically seems to me greatly to illuminate their art. I have tried, therefore, by taking

Auden's major works in turn, to show their relation to his fundamental artistic (and intellectual) concerns, so that the development of his poetry can be seen not as bizarre or perverse but as perfectly consistent. The reader should, after reading this study, be able to go to any work of Auden's and not be puzzled as to what the poet is trying to do in it (though its *detail* may often be perplexing).

My second aim has been to describe the essential qualities of each important work, to provide not a list of its parts but a discussion of the *kind* of work it is, its special qualities of form or feeling, especially its combinations and changes of tone, its structural innovations, its ways of presenting and arranging its human subject.

In attempting to see the general features of Auden's career and of his separate works, I have been unable to analyze any poem or any side of Auden exhaustively or even fully. Some pieces (*Paid on Both Sides*) and some aspects of Auden's work (his criticism, his opera libretti) I have dealt with much too briefly; and, in trying to deal generally with so much, I have had little space to quote the poems and none for extended analysis. But it seems more important, at this point in Auden criticism, to stress the meaning of the *whole* work and the *whole* career; for too many critics have been content to pull out this string or that of an Auden tapestry and complain that its color does not suit them.

Most writing on Auden has been embarrassingly poor. Still, the latest arrival has the benefit not only of the best work done before him, but also of those essays which, despite wrongheadedness, sometimes present useful insights. This survey of Auden's career certainly owes much to the perceptions and information of such good critics as Blair, Spears, Randall Jarrell, Barbara Everett, Richard Hoggart, Edward Callan, and Justin Replogle. Frequently I disagree with them; and sometimes (perhaps fortunately) I have had no space to argue my points, but in general I have tried to avoid the worst fault of Auden's less able critics—the assertive judgment (this is good, that is bad) made from a narrow perspective and without supporting argument.

GEORGE T. WRIGHT

University of Minnesota

Acknowledgments

The quotations from the works of W. H. Auden (with the exception mentioned below) are copyrighted and reprinted by permission of Random House, Inc.

Quotations from poems not included in Random House collections are reprinted by permission of Curtis Brown, Ltd.

Passages from Christopher Isherwood's *Lions and Shadows* are reprinted by permission of the publisher, New Directions Publishing Corporation. Copyright 1947 by New Directions.

Passages from Stephen Spender's *World Within World* (New York: Harcourt, Brace & World, 1951) are reprinted by permission of the present copyright holder, Harold Matson Company, Inc.

I thank Edward Callan for permitting me to quote at length from his articles on Auden's long poems; and the editors of *Tennessee Studies in Literature* (and the University of Tennessee Press) for permission to reprint, much changed, an article that first appeared in Volume X (1965).

I am grateful also to Leslie Palmer, Mary Stanley Weinkauf, Larry Yates, and other graduate students at the University of Tennessee, who, in seminars on Auden, helped me understand his work better; to the Fulbright Program, especially the Franco-American Commission for University Exchange, which made it possible for me to stay two years in France as Fulbright Lecturer at the University of Aix-Marseille, a position that gave me time to write this book; to the University of Tennessee (and especially my department chairman, Kenneth L. Knickerbocker) for granting me a two-year leave of absence; and, for helping with various problems of research, writing, and morale, to Professor Bain Tate Stewart (of the University of Tennessee), my mother, and my wife.

Contents

Chronology

1907 Wystan Hugh Auden born at York, February 21, third
son of George Augustus Auden and Constance Rosalie
(Bicknell) Auden.

1908 Family move to Birmingham.

1914- Father away at war.
1918

1915- St. Edmund's preparatory school, Grayshott.
1920

1920- Gresham's School, Holt (Norfolk).
1925

1925- Christ Church College, Oxford.
1928

1928 *Poems* (about thirty copies printed at Oxford by Stephen
Spender).

1928- Lives in Berlin.
1929

1930 *Paid on Both Sides* in *The Criterion. Poems,* his first important book, brought out by Faber and Faber.

1930- Teaches at Larchfield, Helensburgh, Scotland; and at the
1935 Downs School, Colwall (near Malvern).

1932 *The Orators.*

1933 *The Dance of Death* (not produced till 1935). *Poems,*
second edition, with seven new poems.

1935 *The Dog Beneath the Skin* (with Christopher Isherwood).
Film work for six months. Marries Erika Mann.*

*Bloomfield gives this date; Spears gives 1936.

1936   Visits Iceland with Louis MacNeice, July to September. *The Ascent of F6* (with Isherwood). *Look, Stranger* (American edition: *On This Island*, 1937).

1937   Visits Spain, January to March. *Spain. Letters from Iceland* (with MacNeice). Wins King's Gold Medal.

1938   Visits China with Isherwood, January to July; later in Brussels. *On the Frontier* (with Isherwood).

1939   Moves permanently to the United States in January. *Journey to a War* (with Isherwood).

1939- Teaches at St. Mark's School, Southborough, Mass.
1940

1940   *Another Time*. "The Dark Valley" (radio play). Becomes a Christian.

1940- Teaches at the New School for Social Research, New
1941   York.

1941   *The Double Man* (British edition: *New Year Letter*).

1941- Teaches at the University of Michigan.
1942

1942   Wins Guggenheim fellowship.

1942- Teaches at Swarthmore College.
1945

1943- Teaches at Bryn Mawr College.
1945

1944   *For the Time Being* (including *The Sea and the Mirror*).

1945   *Collected Poetry* (American edition only). "Sent overseas in April by the United States Air Force to investigate the effect of strategic bombing on German morale" (Spears, *The Poetry of W. H. Auden*, 169). Wins Guggenheim fellowship. Awarded $1000 prize by the American Academy of Arts and Letters.

1946 Becomes a United States citizen. Teaches at Bennington College.

1946- Teaches at New School for Social Research.
1947

1947 *The Age of Anxiety.* Teaches at Barnard College.

1948 "Began spending the spring and summer of each year on the Italian island of Ischia" (Spears, 251). Wins Pulitzer Prize.

1949 Gives Page-Barbour Lectures at the University of Virginia.

1950 *Collected Shorter Poems* (British edition only). *The Enchafèd Flood.*

1951 *Nones.* Libretto (with Chester Kallman) for *The Rake's Progress,* by Igor Stravinsky.

1953 "Delia or a Masque of Night," a one-act libretto (with Kallman). Teaches at Smith College, as W. A. Neilson Research Professor.

1954 Wins Bollingen Prize. Is elected to the American Academy of Arts and Letters.

1955 *The Shield of Achilles.*

1956 Wins National Book Award.

1956- Serves as Professor of Poetry at Oxford University.
1961

1957 "Bought farmhouse in Kirchstetten, Austria, and began spending spring and summer there" (Spears, 257). Wins Feltrinelli Prize (Rome).

1958 *Selected Poetry* (American edition: 1959).

1959 Wins Guinness Poetry Award. Awarded Alexander Droutzkoy Gold Medal by the Poetry Society of America.

1960 *Homage to Clio.*

1961 Libretto (with Kallman) for *Elegy for Young Lovers,* by Hans Werner Henze.

1962 *The Dyer's Hand.* Elected Honorary Student (Fellow) of Christ Church College, Oxford University.

1964 Awarded Honorary Litt.D. by Swarthmore College.

1965 *About the House.*

1966 Libretto (with Kallman) for *The Bassarids,* by Henze. *Collected Shorter Poems, 1927-1957.* Awarded Austrian State Prize for Literature.

1967 Awarded the National Medal for Literature.

CHAPTER 1

The Character of the Poet

WHAT KIND of poet is W. H. Auden? Critics have often condemned him for not being one kind or another, but they have seldom succeeded, even when they have wanted to, in describing the kind he *is*. During a career that spans two continents and several faiths, his poetry has seemed, from phase to phase, to alter not merely its loyalties but its character. Is it really British or American? really Freudian, Marxist, or Christian? Is Auden mainly a satirist, a Romantic, a journalist, a song writer, or what? Every new poem or new style of his seems to challenge what we thought we knew about him. Randall Jarrell, with delicate malice, once placed at the head of an article hostile to Auden a quotation he attributed to Heraclitus: *We never step twice into the same Auden.*[1]

Two or three characteristics, however, seem fairly permanent. For one thing, although Auden, sometimes very obviously, borrows techniques or mannerisms from dozens of other writers, he has to an extraordinary degree the poet's ability to make what he borrows his own, to mold it into something we think of as recognizably Auden. All readers will probably see as essential qualities of his style a quickness and lightness of touch; a cleanness of phrase and sentence; a caustic wit; an ironic hardness that, even as it recommends love as the answer to modern anxiety and injustice, is seldom in danger of sentimentality. At times Auden's wit is so exuberant and zestful as to produce, in the service of the most serious ideas, fanciful and even outrageous extravaganzas. At other times the wit is restrained and the verse austere; his writing achieves an Augustan, a Latin, a rococo, elegance.

But, in spite of the feeling we have of an undeniable precision, most readers of Auden have had the experience, after reading one of his poems, of being thoroughly mystified—the thing doesn't make sense; the point vanishes between two stanzas; and the reader is left with a blurred image, an obscure situation, a half understood, possibly misunderstood point. It may be that Auden intends this uncertainty as a way of saying that, among all our precise instruments for measuring, computing, refining, we still have no sure knowledge of where we are. But among the causes of Auden's obscurity are some which account in large part for both the blur and the zest of his writing: his concern at once with inner experience and with society, his frequent shifts in perspective, his readiness to interpret anything as a parable of human experience, and his tireless experimentation.

I *Perspectives*

Although Auden's poems have always probed the illnesses of modern society, his approach to this subject has usually been through the examination of inner motives and conflicts. A consistent student of the inner life—of anxiety, guilt, fear, self-doubt, anguish, love—he brought himself for a time in the 1930's to maintain that our inner lives could be put right only if certain social changes occurred; but he has always found more congenial the opposing view that, whatever its causes, the center of our *malaise,* as well as the focal point of any cure, is the lonely human being. His work tends to make the outer world symbolic of an inner reality that is the scene of all finally significant action or at least the testing ground on which all action must be tried out and evaluated. Intellectual as Auden's poetry often seems— removed, detached, impersonal—the center of it is nevertheless the inner man who is thinking, feeling, comparing, refining, mocking, doubting, believing. As Auden puts it in a poem of the 1930's: "For private reasons I must have the truth." (*OTI,*° XVII)

Still, from another point of view the *public* reasons are important. Skeptical of utopias, critical of society's administrators and managers, Auden is always alert to the contradictions between the personal and the public; and his poetry constantly shifts its angles of vision in order to show graphically the distance between the feeling inner self and what that self looks like from

°*On This Island* (New York, 1937).

18

the point of view of the state, or of an objective observer. Even such an observer is at successive moments a social scientist, an interplanetary visitor, a psychoanalyst. The perspectives are often different, often changing; but all of them are needed to correct one another, to fill out Auden's view of the whole man: anguished self, citizen, organism, outsider.

Outer perspectives, however, may be fairly clear (although some of their intricate combinations can be puzzling); it is the *inner* perspective that often makes poems hard for us to focus. In the early work Auden uses syntactical ellipsis to give us that hard, gruff, urgent sense of meaning deeper than words: "Can speak of trouble, pressure on men/Born all the time, brought forward into light/For warm dark moan." (*CP,** 24) Frequently, too, both here and later, the syntax, though always crisp, is very involved; in fact, no other modern poet uses such various or such elaborate sentences.

Auden's poems are also full of unexplained pronouns, concepts, jokes, and contexts. Especially in the early poems (1928-32) do we have a decisive sense of something happening, but not in a clearly defined place or time or situation. Many of these early poems revolve around the fighting of some unspecified war or an unexplained exile, but we do not know exactly who the enemy is, or what war we are engaged in, what its purpose is, or what we hope to gain. Although we may sometimes identify the cause with Marxist revolution (and early readers often did), we are not told enough to justify this identification; and the war is usually more intelligible as a conflict between inner forces of a Freudian kind, perhaps between a child and his elders.

This deliberate blurring is necessary to Auden's aims in these poems. The effect is that of dream-symbolism; for Auden, in exploring the inner life, is trying to present objects and events which are strong in felt, not reasoned, significance. What is important in the early poems is not the intellectual exposition of the social or psychological doctrine but the feeling that accompanies ambiguous commitment: what it feels like to go into voluntary, purposeful, if regretful, exile or partly to see one's way out of smothering anxieties and guilts. Even later on, when Auden's poetry becomes more discursive, the inner reality is still

**The Collected Poetry of W. H. Auden* (New York, 1945).

19

central. As with more obvious stream-of-consciousness techniques, Auden's aim is to avoid explaining what the feeling self already knows and he presents landscapes, statements, and dream-imagery as correlatives of inner anxiety or polished corruption. Indeed, much of the best of Auden's work is expressionist in character; and even the rational statements, however analytical they sometimes become, normally function in poetic structures which distort outer reality to conform to the self's feelings of anguish, dread, hope, faith, or worry.

For example, the opening stanza of "As He Is" (*CP*, 179-81) seemed quite opaque when I first read it:

> Wrapped in a yielding air, beside
> The flower's soundless hunger,
> Close to the tree's clandestine tide,
> Close to the bird's high fever,
> Loud in his hope and anger,
> Erect about his skeleton,
> Stands the expressive lover,
> Stands the deliberate man.

Gradually I realized that Auden is speaking of man in general and of the universe that surrounds him: the air that stirs as he moves; the plant life whose thirst, when we come to think of it, is unlike that of other thirsty things in being silent; trees in which the sap rises like a tide (the image echoes one of Rainer Maria Rilke's), but also silently and secretly; birds that seem intense and live in the air above us—hence the pun "high fever."

Later on Auden speaks of this man as

> The brothered and the hated
> Whose family have taught him
> To set against the large and dumb,
> The timeless and the rooted,
> His money and his time.

And, because I have read Auden's essays of this period, I see at once that he is not condemning the strong man's exploitation of the less gifted—"the large and dumb" working class, for example. No, the "timeless and the rooted" clearly refers, respectively, to animals and plants. As with "high fever," the juxtaposi-

20

tion of money and time is a passing joke, which temporarily distracts us from seeing, and later adds emphasis to the fact, that "time" means "conception of time." And when we see this, we see that "money" signifies something like "the human capacity to deal with symbols and hence to develop elaborate social structures," which we then use to lay waste the natural world.

Although all of these phrases generalize certain aspects of air, flowers, trees, birds, plants, and animals, and therefore seem abstract, they nevertheless present these objects from the point of view of the man who experiences them all, who feels the air give way, who is aware of the flower's silence and the tree's unseen activity, who looks up at the bird, who observes the plant's immobility and the animal's imperfect comprehension of futurity. The bird is high, the plant rootless, the animal timeless, mainly in respect to man, so that these descriptions, though abstract, are still expressionist distortions because the point of view is included in the description.

II *Parables*

Another permanent feature of Auden's work is his delight in parables, in all literary or mythological structures that symbolize the relations between parts of the self or the self's relation to elements of society or nature: the unidentified war, the Marxist conception of history, the Christian picture of a world fallen but capable of redemption through miracle. Fairy tales, fantasies, dreams, or any stylized model of events may express for him certain fundamental spiritual conditions in the life of men for which he is always seeking analogues and symbols—the relations between members of a family, between master and servant, between doctor and patient, or the relations that hold in quests, in detective stories, in legends and landscapes.

Auden thus subordinates the usual practical, objective categories of value, of time, and of political order in favor of a world of parabolic relationships that are symbolic of real but inner conditions. He subordinates appearance to what he feels is deeper reality. The surfaces of life are still important to him, for it is through the physical and the immediate that a man works out his salvation. But, although in Auden's perspective one actual event may be empirically more important than another, *any* apparently trivial object, action, or system of relationships—a room, a meal, a forest—may have a capacity for illuminating our lives far beyond what we would expect from its modest position in ordinary life.

Holding such a view, Auden is remarkably attentive to the surfaces of ordinary life; for anything may, if we look at it right, suddenly glow with meaning. Looking at it right involves submitting it to sometimes bizarre perspectives, deliberately deranging our usual rational or sensory categories—having Caliban talk like Henry James, or locating a pastoral poem in a city bar. This kind of derangement is constant in Auden; it enters almost always into his imagery and is largely responsible for the blur of meaning that both intrigues and perplexes. It reminds us that his poetry, however rational in tone and structure, is faithful to its source in that unconscious that never gets logical categories straight; that his verse is often wildly playful and that he is hopelessly in love with variety, improvisation, experiment.

III Play

Experiment, like other important things, may look trivial at first, may be so at first; but the trivial may lead us to the richest sort of meaning. Auden's experiment often begins in parody and ends in conversion; indeed, Christopher Isherwood recalls in his autobiographical Lions and Shadows[2] how Auden (whom he calls "Weston") used to change his personality with his hats:

> There was an opera hat—belonging to the period when he
> decided that poets ought to dress like bank directors, in
> morning cut-aways and striped trousers or evening swallow-
> tails. There was a workman's cap, with a shiny black peak,
> which he bought while he was living in Berlin, and which
> had, in the end, to be burnt, because he was sick into it one
> evening in a cinema. There was, and occasionally still is, a
> panama with a black ribbon—representing, I think, Weston's
> conception of himself as a lunatic clergyman; always a
> favourite role. (188-89)

On a bus trip into the country one day in 1926, Auden embarrassed Isherwood not only by his hat (which raised snickers) but also by his pretentious pronouncements

in resonant Oxonian tones: "Of course, intellect's the only
thing that matters at *all*. . . . Apart from Nature, geometry's
all there *is*. . . . Geometry belongs to man. Man's got to assert
himself against Nature, all the *time*. . . . Of course, I've absolutely no use for colour. Only form. The only really exciting
things are volumes and *shapes*. . . . Poetry's got to be made
up of images of form. I hate sunsets and flowers. And I
loathe the *sea*. The sea is formless. . . . (189)

But, Isherwood tells us, such pomposities "never for a moment
made me feel that Weston himself was a sham. He was merely
experimenting aloud; saying over the latest things he had read
in books, to hear how they sounded." (190) And Auden has
continued to do so throughout his poetic career. He mimics the
tones, the verbal habits, even the imagery of other writers, of
older verse forms, and of political, scientific, or religious points
of view. But this mimicking is not always, or even typically,
hostile. It may even be, at first, a form of reverence, an awe-
stricken trying on of a new hat to see what it feels like on the
head. And who knows? The hat may turn out to fit, to be the
right one for the experimenter. Without the experiment, he might
never have found the hat. Several of Auden's poems in 1939 and
1940 show him "trying on" Christianity before he actually became
a Christian. As he states in *The Age of Anxiety*, "Human beings
are, necessarily, actors who cannot become something before
they have first pretended to be it . . ." (109)

But trying on a hat—or a style or a Church—whatever its serious
side, is also amusing; and, as one of the age's great wits, Auden
is rarely far from a joke. The jokes sometimes undermine serious
purposes, and his poems of the 1930's in particular often suffer
from an uncertainty of feeling: there are too many tones, and
we don't know how to take them. Any sincere stance Auden as-
sumes in a poem—Freudian, Marxist, or even Christian—is always
in danger of being ridiculed by that other, comic side of him.
And perhaps his most remarkable achievement is that, despite
his almost unmanageable multiplicity of attitudes, he has not
wasted his talents in ironic play but has worked through to new
forms, new ironic structures, which do justice to the critical
qualifications of the ironic intelligence, and yet affirm.

Auden, then, is a thoroughly serious poet, and a thoroughly
amusing one. Never only one thing at once, he keeps shifting

his own perspectives on the world and, in the process, reveals different sides of himself. His formal variety is astounding: he performs authentically as satirist, song writer, epigrammatist, didactic poet, meditative poet, elegist, odist; in long lines or short, sonnets or sestinas, octosyllabic couplets or four-stress alliterative verse, loose meter or strict, iambics or syllabics, and all kinds of rhyme. He develops styles and abandons them, a sign not of instability but of versatility—of wide, deep, and various interests. From the oracular early poems to the more direct analyses of social illness; from the quiet music of the early songs to the abstract imagery of the later 1930's that culminates in the earnest poems on Yeats and Freud; and from these to the elegance of "New Year Letter" and *The Sea and the Mirror*, and to the balanced Latin opulence of his more ambitious poems of the last two decades, Auden's poetry is continually changing.

Within these periods, even within single poems, the poetry is rarely single; it plays off mood against mood, reinforces wisdom with wit, enriches its textures with quick changes in feeling. For art, to Auden, is a mixed, a paradoxical, affair. It is play, but play is worth dying for (*DH**, 89); and yet it is, too, "in the profoundest sense, frivolous. For one thing, and one thing only, is serious: loving one's neighbor as oneself."[3] Auden's poetry keeps bringing together the sense of everything as of intense significance, and the sense of everything as trivial and frivolous. But each attitude is coherent only in the light of the other.

In fact, as it explores both the rationalities and suddennesses of the inner life, Auden's poetry asserts as its basic insight the connectedness of everything, even of the most unlikely things. The techniques of wit, the shifting images, the unexpected turns that the prosody often takes, all stress the surprise that life is— "O what authority gives/Existence its surprise?" (*CP*, 351)—its playfulness, its magic, its outlandish order. Inner life and outer spectacle, landscape and self, society and feeling—all are discovered to be connected in mysterious, puzzling, disturbing, yet marvelous ways.

Indeed, the world, touched anywhere, will expose these underground connections—if they are approached with just the right attitude of serious play. Words, ideas, feelings are fun to fool

The Dyer's Hand (New York, 1962).

24

around with, to arrange, to order. They are the landscape of this world, whether it be Freud's or God's; and Auden has always loved to name, to map, and to anatomize this landscape. Ultimately, this kind of happy tinkering amounts to reverence: to enjoy the world is perhaps to make the most pious use of it. As Auden's career has proceeded, he has passed from the nightmare conception of man divided from his own best self by overpowering shadows to the more sanctified fairy tale of man born to evil but capable of enchantment by Grace. Freudian inquisitor and Marxist prophet give way to the more congenial role of ashamed but hopeful Christian.

In the new perspective, achieved by incongruities, even the wittiest poem is an act of joyful obeisance before this astonishing and beneficent arrangement of the world. "Whatever its actual content and overt interest," said Auden in 1956 (in his Inaugural Lecture as Professor of Poetry at Oxford University), "every poem is rooted in imaginative awe. Poetry can do a hundred and one things, delight, sadden, disturb, amuse, instruct—it may express every possible shade of emotion, and describe every conceivable kind of event, but there is only one thing that all poetry must do; it must praise all it can for being and for happening." (*DH*, 60)

CHAPTER 2

First Things

TO ENTER the world of Auden's poetry, we do well to understand another distinction he makes in his Oxford lecture—the distinction between sacred or profane beings or events. "Sacred" beings and events are those that arouse involuntary awe in us, that seem overwhelmingly significant, though often for reasons too deep for us to analyze; everything that does not have this character is "profane."

> Some sacred beings seem to be sacred to all imaginations at all times. The Moon, for example, Fire, Snakes and those four important beings which can only be defined in terms of nonbeing: Darkness, Silence, Nothing, Death. Some, like kings, are only sacred to all within a certain culture; some only to members of a social group . . . and some are only sacred to a single imagination. . . . One cannot be taught to recognize a sacred being, one has to be converted. (*DH*, 55-6)

It should be clear that these terms have here no religious connotations at all. Atheists have their sacred beings just like pious Christians. And any poet during his career follows a trail of sacred beings and events—the characteristic images, attitudes, and worlds that seem to him most meaningful. Even certain forms and techniques, certain kinds of verbal gesture, may acquire their own sacredness. As this study proceeds, we shall try, therefore, to follow the ideas, forms, textures, and kinds of encounters that have been successively or continuously sacred to Auden.

I *How to Become a Poet*

Auden began writing poetry at fifteen "because," he tells us, "one Sunday afternoon in March 1922, a friend suggested that I should: the thought had never occurred to me." (*DH*, 34) Until then his interest had been mainly in science, especially in mineralogy; but, in looking back later, as he reports, he realized that he "had read the technological prose of . . . favorite books in a peculiar way. A word like *pyrites,* for example, was for me, not simply an indicative sign; it was the Proper Name of a Sacred Being, so that, when I heard an aunt pronounce it *pirrits,* I was shocked." (*DH*, 34)

Auden's father was a distinguished and scholarly physician who, the year after Auden's birth in York in 1907, "became Medical Officer and Professor of Public Health in Birmingham University;"[1] Auden's mother was a trained nurse. The youngest of three brothers, Auden grew up reading fairy tales and Northern sagas, of which his father, conscious of his Icelandic ancestry, was fond. Auden later dedicated *Letters from Iceland* to his father and wrote of him: "Some of the most vivid recollections of my childhood are hearing him read to me Icelandic folk-tales and sagas, and I know more about Northern mythology than Greek." (214)

His scientific passion and the habit of fantasy combined to produce what Auden has called

> a kind of daydreaming that was of immense importance to my childhood. Between the ages of six and twelve, I spent a great many of my waking hours in the construction and elaboration of a private sacred world, the basic elements of which were a landscape, northern and limestone, and an industry, lead mining. In constructing it, fantasy had to submit to two rules. In deciding what objects were to be included, I was free to select this and reject that, on condition that both were real objects (two kinds of water turbine, for instance, which could be found in textbooks on mining machinery or a manufacturer's catalogue); I was not allowed to invent one. In deciding how my world was to function, I could choose between two practical possibilities (a mine could be drained either by an adit or by a pump), but physical impossibilities and magic means were forbidden. It is no doubt psychologically significant that my sacred world contained no human beings.[2]

All these early interests have left their marks on Auden's poetry, and they help to account for its basic images and situations. The fairy tale and the saga serve as symbolic frameworks for Auden's intellectual parables; so does the anatomized landscape in which scenes or topographies have their symbolic implications. And the habit of medical diagnosis, the probing of contemporary illness, along with a certain amusement at or contempt for the too easy, too smug, pronouncement of disease or remedy, can be traced throughout Auden's career. In all these modes the stress falls on clear outlines and decisive action.

Perhaps, too, as Monroe Spears suggests,[3] the main problem of Auden as a poet, especially in his early work, has been to strike a balance between rational diagnosis (that of the doctor and scientist) and the construction of fantasies (saga-like conflicts and exiles, fairy-tale quests and punishments, and obscurely significant landscapes). The fantasies always tend, however, to be descriptive of actual situations; (for fantasy to Auden is a method of diagnosis, not an escape from, but a revelation of, the actual.) Realism interests him little; even the novels that most intrigue him are those that can be read parabolically, like fairy tales—Kafka, Dickens, Faulkner, detective stories, late Henry James, and such. For nothing reveals so much about people as fantasy: Touchstone's words to Audrey, "The truest poetry is the most feigning," provide the title for a poem in *The Shield of Achilles* (1955) in which he argues the point.

In his early years Auden also developed a strong sense of musical form. He learned to play the piano with competence, and he sang in school choirs. His musical accomplishments are more extensive than those of any other important poet of our time who writes in English, and this ability is evident in his work. Not only has he produced large numbers of songs to be set to music —and written and translated opera libretti as well—but he has also modeled many of his poems on various kinds of musical compositions, from the oratorio *For the Time Being* to the highly operatic arias and duets in his volumes of the 1950's and 1960's. Indeed, throughout his career his poems have been remarkable for their musical subtlety.

After attending St. Edmund's School, where he first knew Christopher Isherwood slightly, and Gresham's School, where he specialized in biology, Auden went to Oxford, where he soon established himself as a personality and as a poet. His wit and intellectual force made a striking impression on everyone, and he soon became a central figure for those who cared for poetry. Thomas Hardy, his first poetic model, was followed by such others as Edward Thomas, Wilfred Owen, A. E. Housman, Edwin Arlington Robinson, Robert Frost, Robert Graves, and Laura Riding. But in 1926 at Oxford he was stunned by the impact of T. S. Eliot's verse and probably about this time became aware of the work of Gerard Manley Hopkins. With Charles Plumb he edited *Oxford Poetry 1926;* with C. Day Lewis, *Oxford Poetry 1927.* Auden wrote poetry himself, submitted it to his friends, judged their writing in turn, and explained to them what poets they ought to be reading and what qualities they ought to be aiming at in their own work.

Vivid, decisive, unpredictable, Auden seemed to them not always right, but always impressive. Students, like Stephen Spender, who wished to speak with him made appointments as if he were a don; then, "one was liable to be dismissed suddenly and told the interview was at an end."[4] "I was," Auden now admits, "insufferably superior with anybody who, when speaking about matters in which I was interested, said something I thought stupid."[5] Spender, at his own first interview, nervously gave wrong answers to Auden's question about the poets he admired, whereupon Auden proceeded to explain his own more developed point of view:

> He told me that the subject of a poem was only the peg on which to hang the poetry. A poet was a kind of chemist who mixed his poems out of words, whilst remaining detached from his own feelings. Feelings and emotional experiences were only the occasion which precipitated into his mind the idea of a poem. When this had been suggested he arranged words into patterns with a mind whose aim was not to express a feeling, but to concentrate on the best arrangement that could be derived from the occasion. (46-47)

As for Auden's own place in the poetry of the future:

> He thought that the literary scene in general offered an empty stage. "Evidently they are waiting for Someone," he said with the air of anticipating that he would soon take the center of it. However, he did not think of himself as the only writer of the future. He had the strongest sense of looking for colleagues and disciples, not just in poetry but in all the

arts. . . . A group of emergent artists existed in his mind, like
a cabinet in the mind of a party leader. (47)

Isherwood sketches Auden's personality with a freer, more
humorous hand:

> He smoked enormously, insatiably: "Insufficient weaning,"
> he explained. "I must have something to *suck*." And he drank
> more cups of tea per day than anybody else I have ever
> known. It was as if his large, white, apparently bloodless
> body needed continual reinforcements of warmth. Although
> this was the height of the summer, he insisted, if the day was
> cloudy, on having a fire in the sitting-room. At night he slept
> with two thick blankets, an eiderdown, both our overcoats
> and all the rugs in his bedroom piled upon his bed. (193-94)

Isherwood had reticences with his other friends, "But Weston
left nothing alone and respected nothing: he intruded everywhere; upon my old-maidish tidyness, my intimate little fads,
my private ailments, my most secret sexual fears." (194-95)
And C. Day Lewis recalls that Auden's exuberance "redeemed
. . . the dogmatism, the intellectual bossiness, and the tendency
to try and run his friends' lives for them, all of which were by-
products of this excess of life."[6]

Curiously enough, Auden was not militantly rebellious. "He
rejected, quietly and without fuss," says Spender, "the moral
views of both his preceptors and his fellow undergraduates."
(48) His originality evidently never required extravagantly anti-
social gestures of defiance. But he had a force that grouped
people around him, imposed on them many of his own ideas and
even much of his own imagery. In consequence, as Spears points
out,[7] the Auden who became famous as the central figure of his
group in the 1930's did not merely express the general attitudes
of that group; to a large extent he created it and gave it its
images, its tone, its ways of thinking, feeling, and writing.
Although during the 1930's their political positions differed somewhat from his own, they continued to look on him as their most
eloquent, if least orthodox, spokesman. And when he later de-
fected from their views, moved to America, and became a Christian, some of his friends—and many liberals who saw Auden as
the leader of a radical group—felt his change of allegiance to be
a betrayal.

One other important element in Auden's early career was his attachment to German literature and German culture. At the end of his university days his parents offered him the chance to spend a year abroad; and, although most young Englishmen were traveling to France to glimpse "the lost generation," Auden, partly influenced by his enjoyment of Germanic sagas and of Old English poetry, which he had discovered through the Oxford lectures of J. R. R. Tolkien, decided to visit Germany. The effect of his stay there on his poetry and his thinking has been considerable. Although his knowledge of French literature is extensive and "he reads and rereads [Dante] in the original,"[8] he owes much more, as later chapters will show, to such German writers as Rilke, Brecht, Kafka, Freud, and Marx, not to speak of German popular songs, the work of Kierkegaard, and the whole German Protestant tradition.

II *Where Nobody Is Well*

Auden and his friends grew up in the 1920's, an era of widespread disenchantment. They had spent their earliest years in Edwardian England—that well-satisfied, opulent world in which only a few writers and thinkers deeply questioned the validity of the social and moral structures. During World War I, which shook that civilization to its roots, they were children, approaching or passing through their adolescence (Auden was eleven when it ended), not old enough to join brothers, fathers, or neighbors (Auden's father was gone for over four years) in a struggle that made disturbingly clear the disparity between elderly ideals and youthful experience. The poems of Wilfred Owen, which exposed this disparity dramatically, were not lost on young men who later often felt both guilty and deprived because they had missed what seemed the most significant experience of their lifetime.

After World War I the West tried to return to normal and to pretend that nothing really crucial had happened. But if there had been a certain falsity in the prewar smugness, the postwar normalcy rang still more obviously hollow. To many young men like Auden, the claims of almost every kind of respectability and orthodoxy had been publicly exposed as sham; and yet the same old phrases, the same old flags, continued to be turned and waved. The disenchantment with heroic Victorian ideals did not begin in 1914, but World War I convinced millions of English-men that war was not glorious but vicious, not human and heroic but terrifyingly mechanical, not a series of brilliant strokes but a succession of blunders. To the skeptical young, the traditional façade of public ideals seemed to crumble into fragments of empty oratory—foolish and dangerous platitudes still declaimed by the official guardians of a corrupt civilization: the Press, the Government, the Army, the Church, and even Women.[9]

How does one respond to a world governed by values in which one has ceased to believe? Mockery is a possibility; and there is plenty of it in the literature of the 1920's. Eliot may not laugh at the civilization he shows as exhausted, but writers like James Joyce, Gertrude Stein, and Evelyn Waugh show how play-fulness can be turned to serious purposes. All of the Auden group learned at least to be irreverent; Isherwood developed a fine sense of mockery; but Auden became the most playful poet of the century. Deliberately disrespectful, deliberately vulgar, he showed his contemporaries how colloquial language could be used not only to shock conventionality but also to expose and ridicule its sham.

Another natural response is to look for guidance. If the world these young men were entering was not as their elders had described it, who could tell them what it *was?* History seemed to be entering a new phase—the war had perhaps only drama-tized the situation—and it was going to be necessary to re-evalu-ate everything with the help of new lines of thought which were only beginning to make their influence felt. Freudian psychology in particular could throw new light on the nature of man, on the value and function of his social institutions; sociological thought could survey the prospects of individual and national happiness in an industrial civilization productive of both re-sources and problems that had never existed before.

Again and again, therefore, the young writers of the 1930's speak of their world as new—as a new country requiring new people, new signatures, new verse, new writing. They think of themselves as having the right to step forward to condemn and to remake the age, not only on the grounds that the solutions of orthodoxy have been discredited but also because they felt be-hind them the undeniable strength of their own prophets—Freud, D. H. Lawrence, later Marx, and a host of lesser but still cogent minds. "I think continually of those who were truly great," says Spender in a memorable poem; and dozens of his contemporaries did so, too.

It is thus worthy of note that, individualistic as most of these writers were, their attack on orthodox authority was not an attack on the principle of authority itself. Ultimately, Auden and his group almost all came to see that the new prophets also had their weaknesses. But this recognition was, for most of them, a gradual one: what they actually did at first was to substitute a new orthodoxy for the old, a new set of heroes, a different moral discipline, a different rigidity and certainty. For Auden, as we shall see, the new crusading faith is at first the psychology of Freud and Homer Lane, which, by curing individuals, may come to cure the world. Later, for himself to some extent but for his contemporaries even more, the faith is Marxism, the trust in a revolutionary social change that will be followed inevitably by universal human happiness (or at least a good chance for it). The religious faith to which Auden came still later, though again an orthodoxy, is, from another point of view, a recognition that his earlier simple faiths were inadequate, that *human* authorities are all flawed.

Even as early as the 1920's, however, the mythology of "the Auden group" includes not only the great intellectual prophets but also "leaders"—those strong personalities to whom weaker ones look for guidance in their struggle to break free of the murderous conventional world. For the other writers Auden became such a leader, and his own writing is filled with similar figures, anonymous in some early poems but more fully developed in such characters as John Nower of *Paid on Both Sides,* Francis in *The Dog Beneath the Skin,* and Ransom in *The Ascent of F6.* What, in this connection, most differentiates Auden's work from that of his contemporaries, however, is that he usually stresses the weakness of the leader himself. Aware no doubt of a discrepancy between his own role of leader and his inner feelings of anxiety and uncertainty, he presents leaders who are even more deeply and fatally divided in themselves, who are not the Truly Strong Men they appear to be. (See below, p. 67)

For Auden's interest in politics never superseded his stress on individual moral psychology. And, at least to begin with, the rebelliousness of the Auden group was distinctly nonpolitical.

33

As long as the 1920's lasted, and with them a sufficient British prosperity, the dissatisfaction of these young men was more a defiance of elders in general than a rejection of specific social, political, or economic institutions—of which, in fact, they were often ignorant. Auden even claims that people at Oxford University were quite unaffected by world events: "Revolution in Russia, inflation in Germany and Austria, Fascism in Italy, whatever fears or hopes they may have aroused in our elders, went unnoticed by us. Before 1930, I never opened a newspaper."[10]

When they did turn to politics—and for some of them left-wing politics was a childish dream of heroic exile—they felt, with some justice, that they were discovering a new life. The very novelty of so many young men from respectable families taking an urgent but nonprofessional interest in politics gave to their activity the feeling of a crusade. And even during the 1930's the crusade was only partly political, only slightly economic. The essential grievance of this generation was always the intellectual and moral dishonesty of the Establishment. Although many of them later accepted, at least temporarily, the Marxist analysis of this situation, almost all of them ultimately—and Auden more consistently than most—retained much of their individualist perspectives, their primary concern with the integrity of private life and love, and their understanding of the contemporary illness as a psychological and even religious problem.

The illness, in any event, is what most impresses them all. The solution, even when it submits to Marxist orthodoxy, is usually conceived in almost religious terms: it is a matter of unaccountable but irresistible conversions and choices of exile. The new convert must break entirely with the past, separate himself from father and mother, and seek purification in an unknown country where he will find other of the faithful. This myth of conversion,[11] largely developed by Auden himself, though it makes an admirable vehicle for conveying the dynamics of Marxian commitment, was actually used by Auden, before he cared about politics, as a means of diagnosing the *psychological* condition of the modern world.

And of England in particular, "this country of ours where nobody is well."[12] We are all ill and must look for help to the great men of thought, the secular saints. If they cannot cure us, we are lost. And what they prescribe—Freud, Lawrence, and others

34

—is a rejection not of political institutions but of conventional pieties and disguises. The proper Englishman makes an effective public appearance. But inside—and in the anatomy of interior conflict Auden is, among this group, uniquely subtle and penetrating—inside, behind the smiling façade, the sick animal, torn by his guilts and fears, is quietly going to pieces.

CHAPTER 3

Symbol, Myth, and Psyche

THE DOUBLE FOCUS—the concern with the relation between public poise and private anxiety—is characteristic of Auden's poetry from the beginning. It can be seen in his first volumes, which are usually spoken of collectively as "early Auden," and which consist of these works: the small *Poems* (1928), privately printed by Stephen Spender; *Paid on Both Sides*, a charade published in T. S. Eliot's journal *The Criterion* in 1930; the more substantial *Poems* (1930), and its second edition (1933) with seven new poems; and *The Orators* (1932). The imagery and ideas of these works, and their treatment of the inner-outer tension, owe much to three sources in particular: the symbolic method of T. S. Eliot, the mythology of Mortmere, and Auden's reading in psychology.

I *Eliot*

In his poem for T. S. Eliot's sixtieth birthday, Auden, using extravagant detective-story imagery, recalls the 1920's as a time of frightened bewilderment and "drought." At that important moment, he goes on, "it was you/Who, not speechless from shock but finding the right/Language for thirst and fear, did much to/Prevent a panic." (*Nones,** 71) Auden's mischievous tone should not obscure the accuracy nor the earnestness of his tribute. What Eliot did for Auden and his friends, and for poets everywhere, was to develop some of the ways in which language could be used to express the contemporary thirst and fear.

For, from its beginning, from the writing of "Prufrock," Eliot's poetry, like his criticism, rested on a moral analysis of society and its institutions. Eliot's was the first significant modern

---

*Nones (New York, 1951).

European poetry to see man's social relationships not as a drag on his more cosmic connections but as the expression of his moral being. Because Eliot sees man and society as caught up together in a complex ecology, he never repudiates or withdraws from society. On the contrary, society is a serious matter in his poetry as it had hardly been for any poet since the eighteenth century. It is certainly serious for Auden, too. For him, even more than for Eliot, society is potentially admirable; it is properly a source of moral values, a civilizer of men. It goes wrong, of course, but there is no point in fleeing from it in the hope of escaping its basic confrontations.

The language Eliot found for his moral studies of man in society is essentially that of symbolism. In *The Waste Land,* instead of discussing particular governments, cultures, and social problems, Eliot presents a kaleidoscopic landscape of hollow, miserable, lost inhabitants of the modern world. Without personalities, associated with historical and legendary characters who have suffered similar situations, moving before us with the frozen gestures and expressions of people in dreams, these shadowy archetypal figures seem, nevertheless, to be living in the same world we know—they cross the same bridges, walk the same streets, hear the same clocks strike.

The symbolist technique, as Eliot developed it, allowed him to put together fragments of life in which were fused together the immediate and the permanent—to merge in a kind of double exposure the city and the desert, the past and the present, the particular man and the archetype. The perspective such a technique affords is visionary: each object mentioned ("the brown land . . . the dull canal . . . the gashouse") becomes the sign of a spiritual condition; the merest list ("Jerusalem Athens Alexandria/Vienna London/Unreal") suggests a history. And the people who float half-seen through this shadowy landscape of broken towers, falling bridges, and deserted cities are never quite distinct from the world they inhabit. All distinction between public and personal is lost in a haze where everyone is implicated together in the common human loss.

This imagery is the "language for thirst and fear" that Eliot gave his contemporaries, and in his early poems Auden follows Eliot in presenting a decayed landscape in bits and pieces which look two ways at once: inward, to the private predicament; out-

37

ward, to the public condition. Even when the emphasis is more strongly on one of these, the other is usually not absent. Scores of lines in early poems can be read as personal or as cultural commentary: "And leaning asking from the car/Cannot tell us where we are . . ." (*CP*, 23). Or:

> Others have tried it and will try again
> To finish that which they did not begin:
> Their fate must always be the same as yours,
> To suffer the loss they were afraid of, yes,
> Holders of one position, wrong for years. (*CP*, 110)

The strength of this early work often derives from the ambiguity. The lines can be read two ways, and it is often the landscape (site of public conflict or diagram of inner conflict) which mediates between them and seems expressive of both. But if the method owes much to Eliot, the typical Auden landscape in these early days is his own. It is developed, in the first place, with a very different tone—young, surgical, incisive, the directness and authority contrasting oddly (as Barbara Everett has pointed out[1]) with the blurred meanings. And, although Auden's decaying world has the same visionary quality as Eliot's, its furniture is distinctive: a countryside of abandoned mines and power stations, "derelict works . . . strangled orchards" (*CP*, 27-28)— the lead-mine landscape of his boyhood fantasies but in ruin.

Sometimes this landscape also seems very northern, marked with glaciers and blizzards: "The ice sheet moving down" (*1928*,[*] XVIII); "The snowstorm on the marsh" (VIII); "the frozen dam" (IX); "Avalanche sliding, white snow from rock-face" (*1933*,[**] II). The setting seems strange, half known and half envisioned, a familiar landscape but in an unfamiliar context, the scene of a mysterious war whose issues are never made explicit, whose participants even are only vaguely identified: sentries, prisoners, "the trained spy," conquerors, "the dark squadron," a "leader." The commonest emotions felt by the personae are fear, anxiety, guilt, and the sense of isolation or of betrayal.

Although the tone of most of these war poems is serious, sometimes even sombre, what helps to give them their odd effective-

[*]*Poems* (Oxford, 1928).
[**] *Poems* (London, 1933).

ness is the war imagery reminiscent of boys' adventure stories, tales of spies, H. G. Wells's narratives of ruined civilizations, or the war stories of C. E. Montague, from one of whose books Isherwood derived the title of his autobiography *Lions and Shadows.* A still more important source is the tradition of Icelandic saga, to which Auden in the late 1920's introduced Isherwood, who promptly noticed a striking similarity between the heroic Norse warriors "with their feuds, their practical jokes, their dark threats conveyed in puns and riddles and deliberate understatements" and "the boys at our preparatory school." When Isherwood pointed out this resemblance, Auden "was pleased with the idea: we discussed it a good deal, wondering which of our schoolfellows best corresponded to the saga characters. In time, the school-saga world became for us a kind of Mortmere . . . " (192-93).

II *Mortmere*

But what was Mortmere? When Isherwood was at Cambridge, he and his best friend Edward Upward (whom he calls "Chalmers") constructed an elaborate fictional world which curiously resembles the early imagery of Auden. They began with a few isolated figures, particularly with one they called "The Watcher." "We imagined him," says Isherwood,

> as a macabre but semi-comic figure, not unlike Guy Fawkes, or a human personification of Poe's watching raven. He appeared to us, we said, at moments when our behaviour was particularly insincere; one might, for example, be telling a boastful story, or pretending an interest in heraldry, or flattering the wife of a don—and there, suddenly, he would be standing, visible only to ourselves. He made no gesture, never spoke. . . . Mutely, he reminded us that the "two sides" continued to exist, that our enemies remained implacable, beneath all their charming, expensive, scholarly disguises. . . .
> (53-54)

The "enemies" of whom Isherwood speaks are largely imaginary, but they are expressive of the sense of isolation, of resistance to authority, and of nonparticipation in contemporary beliefs and assumptions that led Isherwood to fail his final examinations deliberately and that led Upward eventually to communism. Wherever they walked in Cambridge, they "encountered enemy agents." (67) Soon they hit on the conception of "The Other Town": the notion that, beneath the Cambridge surface that everyone could see, plots and counterplots of an amazing complexity were being worked out. If one knew the right door, one could enter the world behind the town, a world of quietly plotting enemy agents, but also of some who were on the better side, "medieval bogies" and "the ghosts of our favourite writers." (72)

Later the two young men decided that the "Other Town" wasn't Cambridge at all but (and the description reminds one of Pressan Ambo in *The Dog Beneath the Skin*) "a village somewhere among the enormous downs, on the edge of the Atlantic Ocean." (101) They named it Mortmere, and they peopled it with numerous odd characters—the Reverend Welken, who "had been guilty of moral offenses with a choirboy and had later suffered severe pangs of conscience, persuading himself, at length, that, as a punishment for his crime, his dead wife was appearing to him in the form of a succubus" (102); Ronald Gunball, who "saw wonders and horrors all about him, his everyday life was lived amidst two-headed monsters, ghouls, downpours of human blood and eclipses of the sun—and everything he saw he accepted with the most absolute and placid calm" (102-3); Reynard Moxon, who ran a brothel for necrophiles and kept "a large black serpent which accompanied him on rambles after dark" (106); and a whole villageful of similar grotesques.

In Auden's early poetry, as in Mortmere, the fantastic masks the real; and the fantasy gives to the ordinary details of life a peculiar air of displacement, and to the people a quality of disconnection. The comic characters of Mortmere have been treated with that dimming, mythmaking touch of Eliot's; but otherwise we are in the same world of powerful and obscure enemies, wars without explicit issues, Our Side and whatever We stand for (mainly rebellion) against Them and Their abused authority.

III *Psychology*

Still, the Mortmere landscape has become more than a fantasy setting for vague feelings of rebellion. Where Eliot overlaid his picture of the modern world with the anthropological learning of Sir James Frazer and Jessie Weston—an anthropology that looks both into the self and out to the culture—Auden mounts his adventure myth on two other contemporary conceptual images: the Freudian dream and the vision (eventually Marxist) of a √ better world. The one faces inward toward the individual and the past; the other, outward toward society and the future. But each is dependent on the other, each has a view of history to account for the present conflict, and each proposes a cure for today's illness. Marx came later, but Auden's reading in psychology was already extensive by 1928. Hence, while Mortmere in the undergraduate version is a simple game, a framework for continual fanciful improvisation, Auden has deepened the fable by secreting within it a kind of allegorical psychology, by projecting the abstract and inward terms of mental illness and health onto the external landscape of a rather Norse Mortmere.

As Auden diagnoses modern illness in these poems and searches for its cure, he follows his chief mentors of these early years—Freud, Georg Groddeck, Homer Lane, and D. H. Lawrence. The main theme of all these writers, as Auden reads them, is that modern man has lost his capacity for the instinctive life, for the kind of natural and fruitful love that alone can make human √ relationships satisfying. From Freud, Auden derives the fundamental conceptions of the power of the unconscious over the conscious, of the destructive nature of repression and inhibition, and of the lifelong struggle between the death wish and the life instincts (Eros). From Groddeck, Auden draws (and sometimes mocks) the theory that a peculiar force known as the *It* inhabits each of us, and that all illness is the result of the *It's* struggle to keep peace between the individual and his environment.[2]

From Homer Lane, an American psychologist and educational reformer, Auden takes his emphasis on love and his version of the psychosomatic nature of all illness. Edward Upward allows one of his characters to present this view dramatically in his novel *Journey to the Border* (1938):

> "Every disease is a cure if we know the right way to take it. Disease is a result of disobedience to the inner law of our own nature, which works by telling us what we want to do and has no use for 'don't's [*sic*]. From childhood up we are taught that our natural desires are evil, that we must control them, deny them room to grow. But they will not be denied.

41

Twisted, clogged with moralizings, driven back from all normal avenues of development, they nevertheless find a way of asserting themselves, appear in disguise, take on unexpected and abnormal forms—malaria, murder, neurosis, joining a Storm Troop, and whatnot." (137-38)

Under the influence of Groddeck and Homer Lane, the young Auden evidently became everyone's diagnostician. Once, visiting him at Oxford, Isherwood contracted the flu; and he subsequently caught cold at almost every meeting, an affliction to which Auden referred as "the liar's quinsey"—*Lions and Shadows* (217). In fact, he gave Isherwood

a whole catalogue of ailments and physical defects, with their psychic causes: if you refused to make use of your creative powers, you produced a cancer, instead; excessive obstinacy—a refusal to "bend the knee"—found expression in rheumatism of the joints; deafness and short sight were attempts to shut out the exterior world . . . consumption represented a desire to return to early childhood, because the lungs are the first organ used by the new-born baby; epilepsy went even farther back—it was an attempt to become an angel, and fly. (303)

What all these ideas emphasize is the wisdom of letting the life within us have its way, instead of killing or corrupting it by rational control. This point D. H. Lawrence particularly makes—that we think too much and that the stress laid on mind ignores the lower but purer centers of our being, the solar plexus and the lumbar ganglion. The aim is to move with the rhythms of nature—"decent with the seasons," as Auden puts it in an early poem—to lose one's inhibitions, to be "pure in heart," as Homer Lane had evidently been: beyond illness, free to love. And free also to be angry now and then, to loose natural, healthy aggressions. Anger, according to Auden's pantheon, is purgative and good; pity, destructive and sterile.

The early poems present man confronted with his illness and required to choose a cure, to choose between death and health. The present is a time of crisis and possibly of evolutionary transition: man has the chance to repudiate his death wish by developing a higher consciousness, one characterized mainly by love. Usually this possibility is presented through the image of a man leaving his community, striking out blindly on a mission he does not understand but one that is his only hope of salvation. We are made to feel, too, that the burden he carries on his shoulders is not only his own salvation but that of his fellow-men: *someone* must reverse the fatal direction of the modern world by recovering at least his own humanity.

Men of good will, therefore, must resist the cultural practices that tend to reduce the life in them—the deadly clichés of feeling (narrow nationalism, petty pride, "self-regard," provincial and immature emotional patterns) and of language. We are told in *The Orators*, only half mischievously, that the good man should beware all the deadly agents of conventionality, people who have the wrong kinds of handshake ("the marsh—the claw—the dead yam") or who ask questions like, "Am I boring you?—Could you tell me the time?—Are you sure you're fit enough?" (51-52) Healthy people must respond openly to love, without the embarrassments and dodges usual in contemporary life. They must come to see that the illness from which we all suffer is, if understood and properly treated, the first stage of a cure.

The natural, the instinctive, the irrational—these are what Auden, with all his precision, admires and recommends in his early poetry. And the imagery is calculated to support his views, with its mysterious struggle between life and death forces and its investing of topographical strategies with symbolic echoes (faintly reminiscent, perhaps, of *Paradise Lost*). Hence, too, the stern condemnation of evil, the moralistic intolerance of conventional morality. Guilty action and guilty isolation are roundly excoriated, and what Auden in his sometimes pedagogical severity offers to his guilty-schoolboy audience is the path of exile and renunciation—the change of heart that will release man's love.

It ought to be easy, as the schoolmaster's tone suggests. "Man does not choose to love; he *must* love," writes Homer Lane.[3] But, in fact, bad methods of education have so turned us away from the natural and healthy path of love that, even when we come to recognize its superiority, we feel nostalgic for the familiar but deadly life: the past—the conventional, the traditional— is charming in its way, so hard to give up, so richly seductive, even though we know how poisonous it is. "We would rather be ruined than changed": so Auden wrote many years later;[4] and the typical personage in the early poems exhibits the same ambiguous feeling when confronted by the accusing tone of History, Evolution, or Auden.

It is not enough, Auden tells us, to be born handsome or clever or to see what is best to do. Rather, a man must choose his own path, making choices blindly at times but making them always in favor of what in him is most honest and natural. This basic view of the personal imperative is one that Auden speaks of often; and, in his essays of the 1940's and 1950's, it comes to be expressed, in modified form, as a subordination of the Aesthetic and Ethical attitudes to the Religious. (See Chapter 12)

But while Auden indicates throughout his work the honest path that is open to us, he shows us also our inner ambivalence —our wish to be excused from decision, and the difficulty of a firmness that amounts to exile from the normal world of moral slackers. His early poems present this uncertainty in the face of clear (if blind) choices through the imagery of a war played out on an attractively decaying landscape; and the use of this landscape to draw together inner and cultural ambiguities provides him with his own "right/Language for thirst and fear."

CHAPTER 4

The Early Poems

I Poems (*1928*)

Poems (1928), a severe little volume, consists of twenty un-titled poems, most of them obscure. Whether they treat of love or war, the situations they imply are blurred and vaguely tragic. The tone is often elegiac: the war—that northern, saga-like war—is not going well; industry is "already comatose"; and the most vivid figures are those whose deaths or failures are recalled in epic manner: "Morgan's who took a clean death in the North,/ Shouting against the gale, or cousin Dodd's,/Passed out, asleep in her chair, the snow falling." (XIII) But the tone is also frequently accusing, prescribing, condemning, although, to be sure, the speaker is often involved in the general guilt and weakness: "The pointed hand would place/Error in you, in me" (III); "Returned from that dishonest country, we/Awake, yet tasting the delicious lie." (VII)

From our vantage point of decades and volumes later, we can see the 1928 Auden experimenting boldly but not wildly. He is testing tones, combining images and phrases in new ways, imitating the poets he admires, trying to make every line catch fire, every phrase have its effect. His diction is usually simple, sometimes grand, sometimes theatrical. But he reveals himself already a master of syntax, which he manipulates with a free hand, tightening it for effects of tension and hostility:

> Or sit, the doors being shut,
> 'Twixt coffee and the fruit,
> Touching, decline to hear
> Sounds of conclusive war. (VIII)

Or he reduces the language to simple, epic phrases: "But he is defeated; let the son/Sell the farm lest the mountain fall:/His mother and her mother won." (XIV) The strong syntax shows particularly in impressive last lines: "Enough to have lightly touched the unworthy thing" (XIII); "Ears poise before decision, scenting danger" (VI); "Rocks shutting out the sky, the old life done." (XX)

Aside from the occasionally pretentious tone, the most notable weakness is imagery that seems unfocused, blurred, confused. But the successful imagery is the book's triumph. Almost every poem, despite the often admonitory tone, implies some full human situation, from the foggy context of which the poem's utterance emerges. Auden give us glimpses of individuals involved in the predicaments common in adventure novels or sagas; but the predicaments are weighted with what would be for a novel (though not for an epic) a more than usual moral gravity: "Go home now, stranger, proud of your young stock;/Stranger, turn back again, frustrate and vexed" (VI); "Travellers may meet at inns but not attach./They sleep one night together, not asked to touch. . . ." (XX)

Indeed, every landscape no matter how vague and every situation no matter how blurred seem to focus some moral choice or moral failure. The whole book suggests that being human, especially now, is hard work because there are so many ways to fail. It is true that even in the midst of all the moral dangers one may still experience satisfying hours of repose and love (XVI and XVIII), but ordinarily the war goes on. It is a subtle and perplexing war because it is largely internal, and the people engaged in it know themselves so slightly that they may at any moment lose their bearings—by misreading their natures, by being dishonest, by consenting to be misled by the ignorance or dishonesty of others ("lies about the cost of a night's lodging" —XX), or by underestimating the difficulties:

> Nights come bringing the snow; and the dead howl
> Under the headlands in their windy dwelling,
> Because the Adversary put too easy questions
> On lonely roads. (XVI)

II Paid on Both Sides

Six of these early poems were incorporated in *Paid on Both Sides,* a short dramatic sketch about two feuding communities,

Lintzgarth and Nattrass. The setting is in some ways modern, with talk about mills, docks, maps, private flats, Scotland Yard, employers, and pulleys; the characters sail to the "Colonies," send wires, drink sidecars. But Auden's language, starkly elliptical and reminiscent of Old English, transforms the events into a modern-dress Norse saga. As in the sagas, the feud takes its own course, and there is no modern law; the suggestion is clear that in our own day national wars are carried on as senselessly and wastefully as were family feuds a thousand years ago. The verse is sometimes too close to its Old English models, amusingly so:

> Then watchers saw they were attacked
> Shouted in fear A night alarm
> To men asleep Doomed men awoke
> Felt for their guns Ran to the doors
> Would wake their master Who lay with woman
> Upstairs together Tired after love. (*1930,* 15)

But the piece has great vigor. In writing it, Auden gave his extravagance free rein and achieved a humor that is absent from *Poems* (1928). Although the basic situation is tragic, and most of the poetry elegiac, there are funny passages, notably the scene in which the Doctor takes from his bag "circular saws, bicycle pumps, etc." and "extracts an enormous tooth from the body" of a character recently shot. Through such mischievous touches, which give the charade diversity if not coherence, Auden reveals an easy playfulness that he has explored throughout his career.

III Poems (*1930*)

Poems (1930) returns to the serious tone of the earlier collection. Indeed, nine of its thirty untitled poems are taken from the 1928 volume; and the general mood of the new book is not strikingly different, although the poems are more accomplished and less surrealistically disconnected. There are still some private love poems, but the chief thematic innovation in this volume is that the poems as a group compose an urgent diagnosis of England's condition and an appeal, even a warning, in behalf

Poems (London, 1930).

of a change of heart. The Norse imagery is found chiefly in the poems retained from 1928; the new pieces that use the imagery of war, enemies, and the two sides seem more immediate in time and place.[1] The situations may still be blurred, but the patient is unmistakably modern England.

More sharply than in 1928, these poems contrast the mythical and the commonplace. As Barbara Everett writes, Auden's myth "combines an elusive generality with a startling particularity of detail. As in a dream, random details are invested with enormous emotional or psychological importance, though the meaning of the whole is never absolutely explicit."[2] Poem XXIX, for example, gives new significance to such ordinary details as a "cigarette-end smouldering on a border/At the first garden party of the year." The same poem presents commonplace features of English life ("The leisurely conversation in the bar/Within a stone's throw of the sunlit water/. . . those women/. . . in the country parishes") as strategic elements in a mammoth conspiracy. In one poem after another the ordinary is thus suddenly and peculiarly freighted with meaning. The mysterious significances of Mortmere, of John Buchan, or of detective stories are surprisingly and brilliantly used to light up the pervasive guilt, the radical anxiety, of England.

At the same time, it is a mistake to see Auden's criticism as Marxist. Monroe Spears is surely right in stating that the new poems "imply more clearly a social-political theme," but he is surely wrong in considering that, together with the old, they "form an analysis of bourgeois society, of capitalist England." (31) These phrases suggest that Auden is coming to think in economic terms, which is not quite true. Other critics, too, write as if Auden had been a Marxist in 1932, or 1930, or even 1928.[3] But a sounder view is that of Justin Replogle,[4] who holds that Auden's interest until about 1933 is in individual illness or in such illness as a widespread phenomenon and, therefore, as a social problem.

For, even when Auden shows us rich people in this volume—and he does so very little—he does not condemn them for their moral-economic vices of waste or idleness or exploitation of others; he condemns them, as usual, for their inner sickness. The "nonchalant pauses" of the wealthy man-about-town (not a "prosperous capitalist," as Spears says [32]) in Poem IV give a false impression of assurance; but inside he is torn apart, "poised between shocking falls on razor-edge." And the candidate for secret agent who is being tested in Poem I must be willing to "interrogate" the "poises" of the rich: their sickness, not their injustice, disturbs Auden.

What *Poems* (1930) shows is that the whole country, all of Western civilization, is constantly growing more ill, and that the proper cure is a redistribution not of wealth but of health. Such hopes for a new world as appear in the volume are the ordinary ones that young men have of reworking the social institutions they have inherited. Such reform may require surgery, and much that seems attractive will have to go: "We know it, we know that love/. . . Needs death, death of the grain, our death,/Death of the old gang. . . ." (XVI) There will have to be a *social* revolution. But Auden is not yet thinking (if he ever seriously did) in terms of bourgeoisie and proletariat; the war imagery is a metaphor for cultural illness, not a literal description of a political reality to come.

Of course, the imagery *sounds* political; and its very obscurity reinforces the impression that it must *be* political. Decision and action; understanding one's choices and making them; choosing between the old, corrupt life and the new, hopeful one, between death and life—such alternatives fitted the political realm even more obviously than the psychological. Ironically, by the time Auden was ready to write poems announcing a *literal* revolution, he had entirely abandoned the war-poem style that seemed so eminently suited to it.

Nevertheless, Auden's 1930 volume does clearly call on Englishmen to change their world. Poem after poem focuses on psychological illness as a ruinous social fact. Again and again Auden explains (even with a certain glee, as Barbara Everett has pointed out[5]) that there is no escaping the choice of health or illness, the human condition: "Do not imagine you can abdicate;/Before you reach the frontier you are caught. . . ." (III) And he keeps asserting that the moment has come for change: "It is time for the destruction of error." (XVI) This clear certainty, the unmistakable tone of challenge ("Will you turn a deaf ear . . . ?" is the first poem's first line) rings through the whole book and makes a strong contrast with the relative confusion of *Poems* (1928).

But most surprising in this volume is a new sophistication, both of technical skill and of tone. Despite their obscurity, most of the 1928 poems are fairly plain in manner, usually iambic without complication, and declarative if elliptical in syntax; the rhyming and stanza arrangements are fairly simple, the versification conservative. Some more elaborate rhetorical devices occur in the poems later used in *Paid on Both Sides;* and there are some interesting experiments with slant-rhymed quatrains that remind us of Emily Dickinson and with consonance-rhyme (after Wilfred Owen); but there is nothing technically striking or original.

The 1930 volume shows an extraordinary increase in deftness. A number of poems, written in short lines after the manner of John Skelton,[6] reveal for the first time Auden's remarkable skill in manipulating sound and form:

> This lunar beauty
> Has no history
> Is complete and early;
> If beauty later
> Bear any feature
> It had a lover
> And is another. (XVII)

This first appearance of the now familiar Auden elegance is accompanied and consolidated by a new grandness of manner. If the 1928 *Poems* sometimes pointed the finger at the guilty reader, the 1930 persona is more magisterial still: "Since you are going to begin today/Let us consider what it is you do." (III) Sometimes the point is insisted on with mock pedantry: "Love by ambition/Of definition/Suffers partition/And cannot go/From yes to no/For no is not love, no is no. . . ." (X) The tone is that of a schoolmaster pointing out a lesson with a stick; the wit, not exactly funny, is that of the master of whom we are a little afraid. Many of the new pieces are surprisingly abstract, but the abstractness is guarded from possible dullness by the verbal wit, the versifying skill, and the quickness with which the abstract passages or poems are followed by the saga-like landscape imagery.

That imagery is so powerful in several of the new poems that, in giving texture to the whole volume, it obscures the nature of

Auden's development since his 1928 *Poems.* Certainly the imagery is surer; of the ability to endow the commonplace with significance, Auden has become an assured master. But, along with this development of his imagery, the 1930 *Poems* moves clearly in a very different direction—toward wit, abstraction, elegance of manner.

Even the seven new poems which Auden added to the 1933 edition (to replace seven he discarded) show this new elegance. Only one is Norse in manner; only one is Skeltonic and abstract; three effectively combine the new verbal or stanzaic wit with the older symbolic landscape of war and crisis. But thereafter Auden abandoned the Norse saga-style, with its epic tone and its ambiguous myth of a public-private war. The other two fresh poems in the 1933 edition are in a new vein entirely: they ironically exploit the rhythms and idioms of popular songs ("What's in your mind, my dove, my coney?"). Auden thus begins that virtually unlimited mining of the colloquial resources of our time that has been one of his principal trademarks.[7]

IV The Orators

In general, then, *Poems* (1930) is much more poised, more articulate, than its predecessor; the poet is much more aware of the possibilities of both form and fun. *The Orators* (1932) explores these possibilities further. Startling and exciting to his contemporaries, it has been neglected in recent years and disparaged by Auden himself.[8] But, despite its obscurity and occasional silliness, *The Orators* has great exuberance. If the hallmark of the 1930 *Poems* is its movement toward form and elegance, that of *The Orators* is its explosive cleverness, especially its display of Auden's newfound skill at parody.

The Orators: An English Study is a deliberately disjointed series of *tours de force* in prose and verse. The major theme of all the pieces is the sickness of modern society. In these years, as I have indicated, society's illness did not to Auden mean economic injustice or political tyranny so much as the psychological warping of the young. Auden consequently took a strong interest in educational methods and practices, and in the public school system in particular where England's leaders supposedly were trained, where he himself was teaching after his return from Germany, and where one could find all the rhetorical modes, phrases, and systems which were to keep the new leaders as sick as the old. The book, as its title suggests, attempts to expose the national rhetorical structure; to make clear that it is upon this crumbling structure of false ideals, empty phrases, rationalizations and self-excuses that English life is built; and to demonstrate how even the best men, even "revolutionists" in the service of more valid beliefs, may be fatally infected by the insidious poison of the system and destroy themselves rather than it.

In addition to a Prologue and an Epilogue (the first exhibiting the disparity between public performance and private anxiety,[9] the second asserting that action is possible and necessary), the work consists of three sections. Book I, "The Initiates," is a series of prose pieces cast in different rhetorical modes: the address; the prose poem; the litany ("O Bulldog Drummond, deliver us . . . Fair Maid of Kent, hear us"); Gertrude Stein's abstract prose ("An old one is beginning to be two new ones. Two new ones are beginning to be two old ones. . . ."); and the informal letter. The parodies are often delightful; the meanings are not always plain. Still, it is evident that Auden is sympathizing with those who seek a way out of this Babel; but, at the same time, he is showing how hard it is, how all the ordinary verbal routes to clarity and sense are blocked by the ludicrous debris of adult humbug and schoolboy ineffectuality.

Book II, "Journal of an Airman," shows us a member of a revolutionary conspiracy. The miscellaneous entries in his journal include genetic charts, symbolic alphabets, descriptions of dreams, bits of verse, and cryptic notes on friends and colleagues ("Percy is not to be trusted and should be watched"). From this assortment we make out vaguely not only the progress of the revolutionary plot but also the Airman's continuous struggle against such weaknesses in himself as kleptomania, epilepsy, homosexualism, and masturbation—weaknesses that ultimately overwhelm him and lead to his suicide.

The Airman himself is a puzzle: in trying to escape normality and orthodoxy, he enlists our sympathy and is even, insofar as he writes poems and soars above the crowd, an artist; but he is also, as Stephen Spender observes, "the man of action, flying, planning Fascist (?) coups, circulating leaflets."[10] In the context of Auden's and his friends' later Marxist allegiances, the Airman's position as both artist and Fascist is especially perplexing; but again it must be remembered that up to this time in England it was the Fascists, not the Communists, who were demonstrating in public, disseminating their propaganda, and forming what looked like private armies.

Auden's later characterization of the school he went to as "a Fascist state"[11] suggests that insofar as the Airman is a schoolboy and his conspiracy a schoolboy conspiracy, he is a Fascist; insofar as he is in revolt against this background, he is anti-Fascist (though surely not yet Marxist). But his confusion is fatal; he has already been too deeply corrupted. Fascism, it seems, provides no answer to contemporary problems; its appeal is deceptive, its force self-destructive. What the *right* steps are that might change the world for the better, the defeated persona cannot tell us.

Book III, which gives some hints, consists of six odes, experimental in form, mostly celebrating or exploring aspects of the present emptiness and the hope of improvement; but these poems are arresting for their exclamatory utterance, their grim humor, and their private allusions. Spears has noted (35) that, whereas in the 1928 *Poems* the poet speaks always in his own person, in the 1930 volume he uses several personae. In doing so, Auden reveals an immense talent for parody, for catching the tones of virtually any kind of verbal life. *The Orators* shows Auden apparently going wild over this discovery; the book is all parody, of one kind of false rhetoric or another. And the odes in Book III are all extravagant in style as they burlesque their putative models—the dream-vision ("Lo, a dream met me in middle night . . ."); the birthday ode; "The Battle of Maldon"; Pindar; Hopkins; hymns.

In some of these odes and in other parts of *The Orators,* Auden not only parodies a manner but uses it to express his own views. This complex, Swiftian technique, with which Auden has experimented from time to time and which frequently baffles resentful single-minded critics, Auden has employed with great success, notably in the Caliban section of *The Sea and the Mirror.* The double perspective, as it reflects accurately the contradictions of human feeling, makes for an engaging design. "One expects the argument to be ironic," says Spears; "but, with double irony, it isn't." (48) Yet this device does make it difficult for the reader to disentangle what is mocked from what is affirmed.

The difficulties of perspective are especially acute in Ode V (*CP*, 136), which gives a new turn to the usual war in Auden. Ordinarily, that war has two aspects—the young English rebel fights against the Establishment conceived both as a set of external institutions and as a set of responses conditioned by them. That is, both the external enemy and that enemy *internalized* are presented as external enemies in a war. This procedure accounts largely for our sense of profound ambiguity in these early poems.

Ode V, however, shows us a slightly different war, not that of the rebel against *his* enemies, but that of the Enemy against his —the struggle of the conventional, the Conscious, to repress the Instinctive. The battle is hopeless, for the repression of Instinct only results in the conversion of healthy impulses into unhealthy ones: Love becomes Lust; the natural feelings become deadly sins. The effort to avoid this situation, to behave in conformity to one's nature instead of damming it up so that it resorts to violence and perversion, is the basic theme of *The Orators* as a whole. The exuberance of the athletes' ode and the birthday ode; the call for help, bizarre though it is, of Ode VI; the decision of the rider in the Epilogue to go "Out of this house"—all provide partial alternatives to the terrifying self-destruction that accompanies conventional dishonest feeling. It is hard for the crooked to become straight, but nothing less will do.[12]

CHAPTER 5

Hawk and Marx

I *As the Hawk Sees It*

B Y 1933 AUDEN, at twenty-six, was an important poet. His work, though admirably various, was marked by certain distinctive features: a recognizable imagery, elliptical syntax, the schoolmaster's tone, the schoolboy's fun. His career for the next decade or so, long misunderstood, amounts to a rejection of the notion of personal style, a refusal to be limited to a few tones, a few forms, a characteristic manner. In fact, as I have shown, this refusal began even earlier; for each of his first volumes explored a new direction. Throughout the 1930's and 1940's his stylistic experiments continued, to the despair of critics who hold that poets should commit themselves to styles as well as doctrines.

Actually, Auden chose what seemed to him the more difficult way—not to recline against the cushion of a comfortable style, but to knock on as many poetic doors as possible, to try out new forms, tones, vocabularies, imageries, approaches, patterns. The flexibility and the range of contemporary poetry consequently owe more to Auden than to anyone else. We instinctively suspect such a poet of having failed to probe deeply enough the implications of some single style; but, although some of Auden's work has been marred by carelessness and haste, most of his experiments are serious, intelligent explorations of poetic modes new or long disused. Some styles, too, and some techniques he *has* returned to again and again; but he varies them, uses them for different purposes or in conjunction with different accompanying elements. And, finally, it must be said that although poets, especially Romantic ones, usually do develop distinctive styles, there is no rule that requires a poet to do so; that the implications of diversity in style are as profound as the implications of narrowness; and that the personal style to which a poet eventually submits may be stronger for having been long resisted.

Auden's chief reason for avoiding the kind of style that we recognize at a glance—"Oh, yes, that's Browning" or "Obviously Swinburne"—is his lifelong suspicion of Romanticism. The Romantic poet, in Auden's view, thrusts himself into the center of his work, exhibits his private "dementia," makes a virtue of personal confession, and values his own subjectivity not because it tells him the truth but because it is his.[1] The typical techniques of the Romantic poet are self-revelation and symbolism—not the responsible symbolism that we find in allegory, in which symbols are strung together and the suggestions of each symbol are therefore limited to what will go with the rest, but disconnected symbols that are deliberately blurred and left loose to pick up like magnets all possible stray content. Auden admires the unconscious, but not such misuse of it.

In general, therefore, Auden tries to keep his own poetry from being autobiographical in content and from using loose symbols that give us the *feeling* of significance without establishing any precise intellectual connection. These avoidances are by no means absolute, for Auden has tried almost everything. The problem he has set his poetry, however, has very largely been that of remaining forceful and impressive even without these two cornerstones of Romantic technique. By 1933 he must have felt that his poems were often admired for the wrong reasons—for their strangeness and their atmosphere, qualities uncomfortably Romantic. So, rejecting his early symbolic imagery as too charged with unlocated meaning (however allegorical in actual content), he began to search for other techniques to give scope and generality to his work. This search for generality, for largeness arrived at fairly without Romantic cheating (for poetry is always a game and a ritual), is the foundation of all of Auden's work after 1933.

Throughout the rest of the 1930's Auden's writing burst forth in all directions. He wrote satire, ballads, songs, verse of all kinds; he contributed articles and reviews to learned and popular journals; he wrote chapters for books on education, psychology, and literature. He helped to found the experimental Group Theatre, wrote plays for it with Isherwood, and gave it its political direction. Two new journals, *New Verse* and *New Writing*, were founded largely to print his and his friends' work, and one issue of *New Verse* was entirely devoted to poems and essays about Auden. Until 1935 he taught school, first at Helensburgh in Scotland, later at Malvern; giving it up, he went into film work for six months, then traveled—to Iceland, Spain, China— and based two travel books and a political poem on his experiences. By the end of the 1930's, a literary man who had to publish to make a living, he was a journalist as well as a poet; he edited two anthologies of poetry; he taught in New York and wrote as voluminously as ever—books, essays, reviews, poems, a pamphlet on education, a radio play, an opera libretto. His energy was prodigious, and his work sometimes too hurried to be good.

Good or not, its constant aim is scope. Auden struggled to master the largest issues, to understand himself and his times, to see Western civilization in perspective. His prose was therefore full of generalizations about man, art, Christianity; his articles and reviews relentlessly established the contributions of this or that period, poet, or thinker. His liberal-humanist eye increasingly scanned the whole history of mankind and especially that part he knows well—Europe, the West. In 1940 the stance changed but not the large perspective. "What I valued most in Hardy, then, as I still do," he wrote in that year about his boyhood admiration, "was his hawk's vision, his way of looking at life from a very great height. . . ." No one who has had this large perspective "can ever accept either an egocentric, overrational Humanism which fondly imagines that it is willing its own life, nor a pseudo-Marxism which rejects individual free-will but claims instead that a human society can be autonomous." For, to the hawk's eye, "the difference between the individual and society is . . . . slight, since both are . . . insignificant. . . ."[2]

But while the hawk's perspective may confer distance, Auden wished also to stress matters that are within the individual. His art, therefore, continually changes its focus. Like a camera, it moves in from an aerial view to a close-up, moves even up to and through the skin until we see spread out within the self an interior landscape that seems the Platonic source of the one outside. For such quick changes the self often *has* to be generalized—to be not an individual person but a silhouette darkened by the characteristic anxieties of mankind:

And within the indigenous figure on horseback
On the bridle path down by the lake

The blood moves also by crooked and furtive inches,
Asks all our questions: "Where is the homage? When
Shall justice be done? O who is against me?
Why am I always alone?" (*CP*, 8)

Virtually all of Auden's poems look at generalized particulars of human life *sub specie aeternitatis* or, if not of eternity, at least of a very long time. The standard may be that of Evolution or of History as well as of the Christian Eternity. But what is constant is the contrasting focus, moving from inner to social to cosmic framework, from personal to public, from tiny contemporary man to the universal patterns against which man's life makes what sense it does.

II *The Marxist Perspective*

This search for scope, for perspectives on contemporary anxiety, is basic to Auden's work of the 1930's. The Marxist view is merely one such perspective; Auden's devotion to it was never wholehearted and frequently seemed forced and false. The urge to see Marxism as central, to read the early Auden as a social propagandist and the later Auden either as a religious propagandist or as a kind of Grand Duke of Political Poetry in exile, has corrupted criticism of his work until quite recently. Still, he did unquestionably for a time accept the view that, although the main illness of the age is psychological, a political revolution must precede the psychological cure:

> What is the use of trying to remove complexes from individuals when the society into which they will go demands that they should have them? It is no time to talk of educating the young until you can guarantee them security of livelihood, interesting work, and a rational amount of leisure. Goodness knows these alone are not enough. . . . But education succeeds social revolution, not precedes. You cannot train children to be good citizens of a state which you despise.[3]

Justin Replogle has shown convincingly[4] that from 1933 to

1938 some of Auden's poems and plays show two kinds of Marxist influence. The first is that of "Marx the political economist," whose views Auden presents seriously in the 1938 play *On the Frontier* (written with Isherwood) but elsewhere often burlesques. From "Marx the philosopher," on the other hand, Auden derived "the only new intellectual element to appear in his work during the 1930's" (595): "a theory of human nature" according to which freedom consists not "in the dream of independence of natural laws, but in the knowledge of these laws." (587) As man comes to understand the laws of his environment, he can use such knowledge to control it; and *this* kind of control can result in authentic freedom: "But along with freedom goes a heavy burden, the responsibility of choice. Men must choose to learn and choose to control. And at every stage of this process they must choose to act." (593-94) To bring about this new freedom, internal changes in individuals are not enough; spontaneous love is not enough: "Love must be guided by reason." (589)

Aside from a handful of poems, including the impressive *Spain*, only two main works by Auden are, according to Replogle, fully Marxist in idea: *On the Frontier* and "In Time of War," his sonnet sequence in *Journey to a War*. "Most of Auden's works [in this supposedly Marxist period] are not Marxist in any sense of the word." (595) Even the poems that sound like Marxist rallying cries are usually mixed with deliberate or inadvertent skepticism; Auden seems to be trying on, like a hat, doctrinaire arguments, shrill accusations, and arrogantly portentous diagnoses and predictions. In *Spain*, for example, we find an uneasy blend of apocalyptic utopian vision and mischievous playfulness, as Auden hails a future that includes "the enlarging of consciousness by diet and breathing./. . . the rediscovery of romantic love; /The photographing of ravens . . ./[and] for the young, the poets exploding like bombs." (*CP*, 184)

Furthermore, his sympathy for the proletariat was always abstract and remote. Incurably the psychologist, he preferred to probe the inner weaknesses of revolutionists and capitalists alike rather than to describe the happy proletarian world of the future. Incurably the artist, Auden had by 1935 firmly refused to see art as propaganda: "those who come to poetry for a message, for calendar thoughts . . . have come to the wrong door. . . ."[5] Incurably middle class, he tended to think of revolution in terms of its effects on himself and his friends. As he wrote many years later: "Looking back, it seems to me that the interest taken by myself and my friends . . . was more psychological than political; we were interested in Marx in the same way that we were interested in Freud, as a technique of unmasking middle class ideologies, not with the intention of repudiating our class, but with the hope of becoming better bourgeois. . . ."[6]

As the 1930's proceeded, all hope deteriorated of improving the middle class, of preventing war, of finding an answer in communism. Spain as an idea might be inspiring, but the reality —not merely of Fascist but of Communist practices—was shocking: "Nobody I know who went to Spain during the Civil War who was not a dyed-in-the-wool stalinist came back with his illusions intact."[7]

The increasing grimness of the world situation gradually altered the buoyant tone of discovery that had characterized Auden's work of the early 1930's. Even in the mid-1930's Auden's books—*The Dog Beneath the Skin, On This Island,* and *Letters from Iceland*—are full of life and fun, rich in experiment with forms and phrasing. But his style toward the end of the decade often seems strangely constricted. The later plays, the later travel book *Journey to a War,* and the later collection of poems *Another Time* are more sombre than their earlier counterparts. The imagery becomes abstract, the tone impersonal; the writing, though still vigorous, has turned grim and pale. Personifications multiply; persons disappear. A forbidding verse, on the whole—that which Auden wrote in the year or two before his move to America, a period in which, after his extended travels, he had clearly begun to despair of the Marxist answer to human unhappiness.

A more pervasive influence on Auden's work of the 1930's than his Marxism, then, is this increasing skepticism about the power of secular reform to change the world. His verse takes on a new quality—becomes dry, wooden, brittle. But as Europe's immediate prospect grows darker, Auden's perspective becomes more lofty, too lofty to be dominated by any single thinker like Freud or Marx, whom even by 1935 he sees as partial critics:

> Both Marx and Freud start from the failures of civilisation,
> one from the poor, one from the ill. Both see human be-

haviour determined, not consciously, but by instinctive needs, hunger and love. Both desire a world where rational choice and self-determination are possible. The difference between them is the inevitable difference between the man who studies crowds in the street, and the man who sees the patient, or at most the family, in the consulting-room. Marx sees the direction of the relations between outer and inner world from without inwards, Freud vice versa. Both are therefore suspicious of each other. The socialist accuses the psychologist of caving in to the status quo, trying to adapt the neurotic to the system, thus depriving him of a potential revolutionary: the psychologist retorts that the socialist is trying to lift himself by his own boot tags, that he fails to understand himself, or the fact that the lust for money is only one form of the lust for power; and so that after he has won his power by revolution he will recreate the same conditions. Both are right. As long as civilisation remains as it is, the number of patients the psychologist can cure are very few, and as soon as socialism attains power, it must learn to direct its own interior energy and will need the psychologist.[8]

During this period Auden's poetry, like his prose, increasingly aims at depicting the total human situation, on which each great thinker throws his partial light. It achieves this generality through various techniques, the most permanent and pervasive of which is that of dislocation, of suddenly shifted perspectives. Auden dislocates us because he wants us to see something we would miss in its ordinary context, and what he wants us to see is a general truth about life or man or ourselves—perhaps Freud's truth or Marx's but other truths as well, and especially truths that relate one sphere in which we live to others; the public to the personal, the interior to the cosmic or social.

The techniques of dislocation are already at work in the early poetry, and critics have often discussed them. Other procedures for achieving generality have not, until the recent book by John G. Blair,[9] been seen as comprising the central program for Auden's poetry; and Blair's description, though excellent, is not chronological. The next four chapters consider, therefore, the main methods in his search for a poetry that could be large and significant without being self-centered or loosely symbolic.

CHAPTER 6

Plain Speech

A S AUDEN emerged from behind the "Nordic mask" of his
early period, his poetry gained remarkably in openness and
clarity. The private jokes and riddles, the difficult ellipses, and
the unexplained wars and enmities did not entirely vanish; but
other kinds of poems came to look central in Auden's repertoire
—notably, the song; the satirical ballad; and the casual, personal,
reflective poem.

For, under the influence of Marxist social philosophy, Auden
was trying to make his poems more accessible to a wide public.
The search for largeness began as a search for clearness. Although
Auden never quite subscribed to the view of art as propaganda
—and since 1935 has been consistently hostile to the idea—around
1932 his poems nevertheless began not only to explore Marxist
themes but to speak more directly and openly.

Even *The Orators* (1932), obscure as it is, contains some plain,
blunt writing, including coarse invective: "Benthameer, Benthameer, bully of Britain,/With your face as fat as a farmer's
bum." (62) Some of Auden's contributions to the anthology *New
Country* (1933) are also in straightforwardly irreverent English.
One poem is plainly titled, "A Communist to Others." Another,
a dream-vision, presents directly and at great length a satiric
portrait of contemporary England, in such lines as these: "Ram-
sey MacDonald was rubbing his seat/At last he'd been invited
to a Leicestershire Meet."[1]

With such verse Auden is obviously trying to reach a general
audience. And frequently during the 1930's he returns to this
style, or something like it—the direct, arraigning, often coarse
invective. "A Communist to Others," widely reprinted (but not
by Auden), is another example, as is the long "Last Will and
Testament" by Auden and Louis MacNeice in *Letters from Iceland*. In general, the style is unsuccessful—often amusing but

always garrulous. The versifying machine gets started and cannot stop. The stanzas accumulate but do not develop. The fault is common in Auden. His mind, though abstract, is prolific of details and, once put to the task of making out a list, tends to be wildly exhaustive.

The virtue of the defect is that it enables him to try everything, to see schoolboys as saga heroes, to superimpose fantastic Mortmere on actual England, to externalize internal neurosis in landscape or psychosomatic symptoms. The danger of this habit of mind is that the extravagant elaboration of a trivial perception will only betray its triviality.

To be too direct, then, rarely works for Auden, or rarely for long. But he has tried one other device which makes extensive use of very simple language: the mimicking—part parody, part serious—of colloquial idioms and clichés. Taking his hint from Eliot's "Sweeney Agonistes," Auden learned to explore, partly for amusement and partly as a path to illuminating perceptions, the literal implications of ordinary phrases whose full significance we usually fail to notice. A brilliant early example is the song from *The Ascent of F6* in which such common phrases as "Still waters run deep," "there's never smoke without fire," and "there is more than meets the eye" are weighted with Freudian content. (*CP*, 199) A brilliant later example is the "*God only knows*" that ends "The Willow-Wren and the Stare." (*Shield*,* 42)

In most of Auden's poems the banal occurs, if at all, in company with more elevated diction, so that the reader is jolted by the apparent inappropriateness. In "September 1, 1939," for example, when Auden writes, "The unmentionable odour of death / Offends the September night" (*CP*, 57), he refers with deliberate vulgarity to the then current advertisement for a soap that would protect its user from offensive body odor. Such appearances of the banal in nonbanal contexts constitute another kind of dislocating technique: by juxtaposing spheres and attitudes we ordinarily keep separate, they require us, at their most effective, to look more closely at the categorizing habits with which we protect ourselves. As we shall see in Chapter 8, Auden's ballads exploit the banal in similar fashion by using it in a traditional form already loaded with ironic significance. But what about

---

The Shield of Achilles (New York, 1955).

the banal by itself? Can it form the basis of a style? Can it, with its great advantage of clarity, stand alone or almost alone?

I *The Plays:* The Dance of Death

For answer we must turn to Auden's plays where, more than anywhere else, the banal is given extended work to do. The short play *The Dance of Death* (1933) and the three full-length pieces by Auden and Isherwood—all produced during the 1930's by the Group Theatre—are strongly, if decreasingly, influenced by the German experimental theater of Bertolt Brecht. Brecht's "epic theatre" keeps the audience at a distance; forbids it to relax into an easy, irresponsible identification; and aims at inciting it to thought and action. His drama uses popular songs with political content; scenes shift abruptly; characters address the audience directly; and moods change quickly from harsh to soft, pathetic to bitter. Brecht's drama is thus episodic, stylized, didactic; it uses surrealistic dialogue sometimes; and its emphasis is on the social significance of each action rather than on character, plot, or atmosphere. Auden and Isherwood have more fun; but, especially to begin with, their techniques are Brecht's.

The Dance of Death (by Auden alone) is an animated but trivial masque that treats modern society's death wish. The characters are undifferentiated (most are called merely A, B, C, etc.), and they participate in a series of disjointed skits in which the early psychological analysis of social illness seems at last to give way to Marx's social analysis.[2] In this play the banal receives its fullest test as Auden employs it throughout. The result is disastrous. In trying to milk the commonest idioms for their symbolic suggestions, he is often amusing; but the language is too flat and dry to yield much significance. Thus:

> You are responsible,
> You are impossible,
> Out you go.
> We will liquidate,
> The capitalist state
> Overthrow.[3]

In the full-length plays the flat idioms and the beginner's rhymes ("The bus is leaving in a minute:/Those who are com-

ing must step in it"—*Dog*,* [32]) are increasingly subordinated
to other styles that range from prose realism to the poetic
sublime. For the more modest tasks assigned to it, therefore—
patter and chatter and mock self-revelation—the simple colloquial
style is not too unsatisfactory. But Auden does make fewer demands on it; he evidently realizes that, by itself, the loaded
colloquialism, even if everyone can understand it, is too weak to
support much intellectual substance.

II The Dog Beneath the Skin

In *The Dog Beneath the Skin* (1935) the Brechtian influence
can be felt in the abrupt transitions, but the play's make-believe
air largely deprives it of Brecht's single-minded bitterness. Characters and action have almost no realistic foundation. The play
seems hardly intended for actual production, with its cast of
thirty-three distinct individuals, plus Chorus Girls, Courtiers,
Diners, Doctors, Dressers, Invalids, Lunatics, Nurses, Police,
Priests, Procurers, Prostitutes, Students, Waiters, and Villagers.
There is also an obviously unactable dialogue between the hero's
right foot, which "speaks in a cultured voice," and his Cockney
left foot. Through stylized situations and type-characters Auden
and Isherwood survey elements of political reality in the 1930's,
especially the hypocrisy and stupidity of bourgeois society, and
the difficulties of the exile-hero who seeks something better.

Every year, according to the fairy-tale plot, a questing hero
leaves his village in search of the late squire's missing son. The
present quester, Alan, wanders rather aimlessly around Europe
and inadvertently encounters one kind of corruption after another. The modern world is, in effect, shown successively as Red
Light District, Lunatic Asylum, Hospital, and Luxury Hotel. A
kind of Boy Scout hero, Alan manages to remain innocent and
conscientious throughout all his tests by avoiding or surviving
the various dangers which are represented by other characters:
cynical journalists, superpatriotic lunatics, power-mad magnates,
solipsistic poets, the rich who applaud destruction of the beautiful, the lovers who seal themselves off from the rest of the
world, and a mannequin that offers empty heterosexual love. As

---

*The Dog Beneath the Skin (London, 1935).

Alan survives his ordeals, the missing son gratuitously declares himself (an act which anticipates Auden's later view of the Incarnation); and they return to the village, where Alan refuses his reward and voluntarily seeks further significant exile in the company of other men of good will.

The banal style is still central in this play, the norm to which the dialogue and incidental songs continually return: "Speak to me, please, just one little word,/I don't understand you! Oh, this is absurd!" (149) But there is also a great deal of prose dialogue, and prose is used as well for some long set pieces of considerable substance. In addition, lengthy choruses take a hawk's-eye view of contemporary civilization and give dignity and loftiness to what might otherwise seem mere fooling:

> The Summer holds: upon its glittering lake
> Lie Europe and the islands; many rivers
> Wrinkling its surface like a ploughman's palm. (11)
>
> . . . .
>
> A man and a dog are entering a city: They are
>   approaching a centre of culture:
> First the suburban dormitories spreading over fields. . . . (117)

The grandness of the choruses makes an extremely effective framework for the commonplace dialogue. But, even so supported, and reinforced by the good prose passages, the dialogue cannot avoid seeming silly much of the time. *Every* banal phrase does not have a deeper significance; much is mere playful nonsense, as when a waiter directs Alan to the Roof Garden: "Take the lift on the right, sir./At the Fifth you alight, sir." (153) And even the choruses lose their elevation in bathetic or prosy propagandizing:

> Mourn rather for yourselves; and your inability
>   to make up your minds. . . . (179)
>
> . . . .
>
> You have wonderful hospitals and a few good schools:
> Repent.
> The precision of your instruments and the skill of
>   your designers is unparalleled:
> Unite.
> Your knowledge and your power are capable of infinite
>   extension:
> Act. (157)

Aside from the lyrical choruses, the best bits of verse are set pieces (the song of the 1st Mad Lady and "You who return tonight to a narrow bed") in which the diction is also rather literary than colloquial. In fact, in this play Auden, though not encumbering himself with an overstated theory, is in the position of Wordsworth in *Lyrical Ballads*—trying to center his poetry in really ordinary diction, he does his best work in a grander style.

III The Ascent of F6

The Ascent of F6 (1936) is more realistic and more dominated by Isherwood's prose. Instead of a fairy-tale quest, the basic story is a psychological fable, an exemplum about a question that had long interested the two authors: what constitutes real strength in a man? Isherwood argues in *Lions and Shadows* (207-8) that "the truly strong man" does not need to prove himself by heroic conquests of mountains or jungles. On the contrary, it is "the Truly Weak Man" who requires such proofs of his strength, and for him no proofs will ever be sufficient. Michael Ransom, the hero of *The Ascent of F6*, is clearly such a figure. A man of great gifts, a scholar and adventurer, he *appears* strong but actually suffers from a hopeless Oedipal problem. This weakness leads him to attempt the ascent of F6, a strategic mountain whose conquest by a British team will improve England's position in its pointless rivalry with Ostnia.

In agreeing to make the ascent, Ransom plays into the hands of the hypocritical forces that govern modern countries. And, as the leader of his own team, he faces the tragic dilemma of all honest leaders: should he allow his followers to choose their own lives, in which case they will be lost; or should he choose *for* them, in which case they are no longer free and he as a governor will become corrupt? For all government is evil since it "requires the exercise of the human will," which is "from the Demon." (74)

The play is thus extremely pessimistic in its view of society. Someone has to govern, but all who do are corrupt. In the modern world as it is—and no better one is heralded in this play —heroes, and the public that needs them, are equally flawed and equally used and betrayed by their empty governors.

In *F6* the part of the banal style is further reduced. The stylistic norm of the play is realistic prose, and it is mainly the departures from realism that tend to break out into verse—the confrontations (essentially interior) between Ransom and his mother, a few songs, one hawk's-eye chorus, and, most notably, the choral subplot in which Mr. and Mrs. A., representing ordinary people, review public events and private emptiness, often in the familiar banal style: "Home to supper and to bed./It'll be like this till we are dead." (180) Since the ordinary development of this play is accomplished in prose dialogue, the flat style can be used sparingly and for special effects—for example, to underscore points about cultural drought.

But the implication is that flatness, in this form at least, can serve no larger purposes. When Mr. and Mrs. A. become really eloquent, they do so by leaving their average characters behind them, and their average diction as well. The stylistic separation of powers—prose for development, poetry for distance and innerness—fails because the different perspectives are not fused or focused, as they are to a greater extent in *Dog*. Auden's early imagery (and his later imagery as well) keeps looking two ways at once; in *F6* the modes of speech merely follow one another, blankly. And the flat and simple style fails to achieve largeness because it can say only one thing at a time.[4]

IV On the Frontier

In *On the Frontier* (1938) the verse has still less to do. Neither fairy tale nor fable, this play is a Shavian (and Marxist) investigation of the dynamics of public opinion and ignorance that leads to war. Ostnia and Westland (read, no doubt, Waste Land) are the two countries in question, and in each country we see one family of "ordinary decent people" brought by propaganda to hate the rival country. As Replogle puts it, the play shows how everyone—leaders and people alike—"misunderstands what is happening because each sees the world in terms of the conventional cultural framework which created his view in the first place." (591)

As in *F6*, we oscillate between a set of public figures and the ordinary people, but this time *both* groups are developed realistically (except for the device of dividing the stage and showing both families simultaneously). Furthermore, both groups speak prose. Verse occurs only between the scenes, in a few songs, and in the speeches of the two young people, one from each family, whose love affair is frustrated by the foolish war between their countries. Except for the ballads (see Chapter 8), the verse seems perfunctory—as if, with Isherwood's prose realism taking over, Auden had lost interest in the project. The result is, at times, bathos:

> But I was wrong. We cannot choose our world,
> Our time, our class. None are innocent, none.
> Causes of violence lie so deep in all our lives
> It touches every act.
> Certain it is for all we do
> We shall pay dearly. (120-21)

Certain it is, indeed. Since the play seems to show almost everyone's stupidity or shortsightedness, the lovers lack conviction when they suggest that, under Marxism, "the will of love" (122) would be done. Like the other plays and like most of the propaganda poetry of the 1930's, including Auden's, the play is effective when it attacks and caricatures, but not when it presents as a political possibility a never-never land of happy lovers and workers.

Thus, Auden's extended attempts to use ordinary language in all its flatness are not very successful. Amusing lines and even some faintly moving passages—these are the best the style can offer. The concern to attract an audience leads Auden and Isherwood to write more and more realistically and more and more prose. To be sure, Auden has written some of his later poems in flat language, some of them quite successful, notably the two poems "Law like Love" and "Hell" in *Another Time* (1940):

> Others say, Law is our Fate;
> Others say, Law is our State;
> Others say, others say
> Law is no more
> Law has gone away. (*CP*, 75)

But this language is really more than flat; it has a childish ring to it, yet the concepts summed up in the childish tone are abstract and complex. "Law is our State" is not the way ordinary people who believe it would actually put it. On the whole, Auden's experiments with very plain language taught him that plainness by itself is not enough; that prose, on the whole, can do the plain job better; and that other poetic ways of achieving largeness promised more.

CHAPTER 7

The Casual Style

I On This Island

O F ALL the styles Auden developed in the 1930's, the casual, open style was perhaps the most attractive. It is also central in Auden's *oeuvre* as no other style is, for in one form or another he has continued to use it throughout his career. As it begins, in 1933 or so (my first example appeared in the 1933 *New Country*), it is buoyant, clear, and surprisingly personal:

> Now from my window-sill I watch the night,
> The church clock's yellow face, the green pier light
> Burn for a new imprudent year;
> The silence buzzes in my ear;
> The jets in both the dormitories are out. (*CP*, 83)

By 1936, when he put together his next collection, *Look, Stranger!* (American edition: *On This Island*, 1937), he could include some eight or ten poems written in this style, which, together with the dozen songs, dominate the volume of thirty-two poems and give it an entirely different feeling from the earlier collections. The Nordic mask has disappeared, and there is only one poem in the Skeltonic style. Auden is now a public poet, a man speaking with relative clarity of contemporary events and choices, sometimes writing quite directly of himself and his friends and the historical crisis:

> Now north and south and east and west
> Those I love lie down to rest . . . (*CP*, 96)

> And I, each meal-time with the families,
> The animal brother and his serious sister,
> Or after breakfast on the urned steps watching

> The defeated and disfigured marching by,
> Have thought of you, Christopher, and wished beside me
> Your squat spruce body and enormous head. (*OTI,* XXX)

In such poems the setting is often specified, the old elliptical speech gives way to a more traditional sentence structure, and the ideas are clearer and more accessible. Even in poems less personal and less clear the discussion of contemporary events is warmed by the sense we have of a worried man talking, trying to figure things out.

The style reflects Auden's search in these years for "lightness," for the kind of verse in which the poet can talk to an audience easily about things that he and they are both interested in. The alternative, as he tells us in his introduction to *The Oxford Book of Light Verse* (1938), is that Romantic verse in which the poet is "acutely aware of himself as the poet" (ix) and consequently cannot talk easily with his readers. In their progressive alienation from common humanity, the Romantics followed Milton, who was probably "the first to make a myth out of his personal experience, and to invent a language of his own remote from the spoken word" (xi)—as Auden himself had done in his early verse. "Lightness" is preferable to that, but it often requires a personal voice. It poses to Auden, therefore, some crucial questions: How personal can one be in a light poem without indulging in Romantic autobiography? And can one be light and still profound, still deal with complex ideas?

The first question is a delicate one, indeed. Above all, Auden wants to avoid the kind of verse in which the poet says in effect, "Look at me! Isn't my illness fascinating?" and proceeds to describe the symptoms. Can one use oneself in poems at all without falling into this trap? Well, Yeats did so, and many of the poems in *On This Island* recall his casual reflective style. The essential thing, though, for Yeats and for Auden, is to pass from the immediate personal situation to the more general, to *use* the personal as a way of getting to what is *really* important. In the gross particulars out of which one's own life is made, one discerns general principles, general truths and patterns.

So in the poem that begins, "Now from my window-sill . . ." Auden quickly moves, in the second stanza, to the town and beyond, and, in the third, both farther out to a cosmic perspective and further in, to the inner human being—not himself but

71

anyone. His own personal life does not quite get into the poem, only the life of the town and the school: "Preserve our Provost, Piermaster, Police/ . . . To these players of badminton to-night,/ To Favel, Holland, sprightly Alexis give."[1] Auden is trying to establish his speaker in an actual human environment, as Yeats often surrounds himself with cultural or country figures.

But, even after writing such lines, Auden is suspicious of them: the first of the three lines above appeared in *New Country* but did not survive even until *On This Island;* the last two got that far but no farther. The original eighteen-stanza poem, in fact, has been cut to eight in recent collections, and the stanzas lost include all of those which once contained local details. The resulting poem is far more austere and impersonal than the earlier versions.

Much of Auden's later verse, nevertheless, continues to be written out of his personal situations, although the poet's self rarely intrudes very far and serves mainly as a characteristic self. The situations he writes about are those in which the poet can function as "anybody"—waking up, feeling lazy, being tempted, falling in love. What he explores in such situations are not the respects in which W. H. Auden's reactions are different from everyone else's, and more intriguing, but the respects in which his perceptions and responses are normal, are human, and tell us something about man in general. The speaker of the personal poems is, therefore, a man, an intelligent man, who yet makes no extravagant claims. He is a man speaking to men, but not, as in the Wordsworthian version, a better and more sensitive man than his listeners. He is just someone who knows how to talk in verse.

But can he, while speaking easily, say anything important? Auden's practice suggests both that he can and that he can't. The casual poems of *On This Island* frequently make points that are not at all easy to grasp. Even the relatively popular verse form of "Now from my window-sill" or of "Out on the lawn I lie in bed,/Vega conspicuous overhead/In the windless nights of June . . ." (*CP*, 96) gives way, in later poems of the same group, to more complex forms that present more elusive ideas:

> Your portrait hangs before me on the wall,
> And there what view I wish for I shall find,

72

> The wooded or the stony, though not all
> The painter's gifts can make its flatness round;
> Though each blue iris see the heaven of failures,
> That mirror world where Logic is reversed,
> Where age becomes the handsome child at last,
> The glass sea parted for the country sailors (*CP*, 114)

There seems to be too much to say for *very* plain speech; irony and indirection are too valuable to do without, even when one knows that with every use of them the audience is dwindling, the light style gaining perhaps not the right kind of weight.

In *On This Island* Auden wishes, after all, to discuss some complex questions. The volume places before us the choice between the crooked, private, solipsistic love that is a death wish in disguise and the disciplined love that leads to action, knowledge, control of the world, and freedom. So one casual poem, in not so casual English, states:

> Yours is the choice, to whom the gods awarded
> The language of learning and the language of love,
> Crooked to move as a moneybug or a cancer,
> Or straight as a dove. (*OTI*, XXI)[2]

The two loves are not always easy to tell apart; but when the terms are political, the forces of death are those of the status quo; the forces of life call for a new world, condemn dictators and militarists, and resist those who love death.

If these ideas are not extraordinarily hard to grasp, they are nevertheless developed with considerable ingenuity. Auden's poetic intelligence—consistently juxtaposing and superimposing disparate elements, shifting perspectives, and providing new contexts (linguistic, physical, and social) for familiar objects, persons, and practices—tries to show us the world in which we live, a complex world further complicated by changes in our own ways of seeing it. The plainest English is simply not up to the job of showing all this. What seem like clear ideas get awfully intricate when we look at them closely. For the poet's material consists not only of life as we lead it but of life as we watch ourselves leading it; and this extra dimension, a gift of Romanticism which we cannot ignore, makes authentic simplicity impossible.

So in Auden's practice the poems that retain the casual manner are often not easy to read. The warm, personal speech is balanced by the complexity of the perception that we see the persona working out. The syntax becomes playful—"Easily, my dear, you move, easily your head" (*CP*, 36)—or ambiguous: "Looking and loving our behaviours pass/The stones, the steels, and the polished glass . . ." (*CP*, 36) And the most powerful images are often those that escape rigid adherence to logical categories, that mix metaphors boldly:

> In the houses
> The little pianos are closed, and a clock strikes.
> And all sway forward on the dangerous flood
> Of history, that never sleeps or dies,
> And, held one moment, burns the hand. (*OTI*, XXX)

This is plain enough in its way, but surrealistic; as usual in Auden, the poem looks two ways at once—toward the rational imperatives of history and toward the irrational impulses of the unconscious.

Thus, the poems in *On This Island* are often less clear than they at first seem, and perhaps intentionally so. For, since Auden is trying to fuse the rational and the instinctive, if the poem were too clear it would be false to this double source of modern life. So the imagery is often elusive, the abstractions confusing; key words, recurring often, seem to have private meanings. The riddling Rilkean sonnets, and the sestina "Hearing of harvests," with their surface clarity and their hidden significance, carry farther this curious tendency to give and to withhold, to expose and to conceal, to speak distinctly but in code. The casual style is casual only in tone; as with Yeats's poems in the same genre, the warm and winning manner turns out to belong to a highly developed intellect, and what may be casual for him is hard work for the reader.

In fact, the combination of casual tone with diction a little elevated is characteristic of Auden's poems throughout the 1930's. One of their strengths is the ease with which the casual manner gives way to the prophetic, thereby suggesting that absolute and apocalyptic reality which lies just beneath our ordinary life. Anything can happen and probably will—so Auden's poetry continually tells us with its styles as well as with its words. Some poems of the 1930's are completely prophetic in manner, like the

"Prologue" to *On This Island* (*CP*, 89-90); others, often written in a kind of Latin Alcaic meter (usually four lines, the first two longer than the last two), use conversational expressions but maintain some distance from the casual tone—"Journey to Iceland" or "Epilogue." (*CP*, 7-9; 25-26) And this technique, developed throughout the 1930's, leads Auden to his main stylistic solution of the problem: the syllabic poems that dominate his later work and that drench exceedingly complex speech in disarmingly casual tones. The agreeably chatty poems of *On This Island* prepare us for the openly cryptic style of the last two decades (see Chapter 16).

II Letters from Iceland

It would be ungrateful, however, to overlook the last and most impressive monument of the pure casual style, the charming *Letters from Iceland*. This miscellany tries to avoid the dull repetitiousness of most travel books in which "the actual events are all extremely like each other—meals—sleeping accommodation—fleas—dangers, etc." (142) Instead, the book is an engaging hodgepodge of letters in prose and verse, photographs, travel tips, amusing quotations from former visitors, and a poetic "Last Will and Testament" in joint doggerel by Auden and his collaborator, Louis MacNeice. Most of the writing, however, is Auden's; and, though it includes some fine serious poems, its general mood is lively and witty. In particular, the "Letter to Lord Byron," its parts scattered throughout the volume, is brilliantly Byronic, full of absurd polysyllabic rhymes and delightful chat—more about books and authors and Auden and England than about Iceland. Here Auden writes about Jane Austen:

> You could not shock her more than she shocks me;
>   Beside her Joyce seems innocent as grass.
> It makes me most uncomfortable to see
>   An English spinster of the middle class
>   Describe the amorous effects of "brass,"
> Reveal so frankly and with such sobriety
> The economic basis of society.[3]

This is charming verse, and it abounds in "Letter to Lord Byron." But the form was too loose for Auden to continue using it; it encouraged laxness and empty facility. And Auden's genius depends on his continuing to explore increasingly subtle forms.

The whole book, however, is more subtle in form than it appears. It is a collage,[4] loosely strung together on the thread of the "Letter to Lord Byron," which Auden conceived as "a description of an effect of travelling in distant places which is to make one reflect on one's past and one's culture from the outside." (141) As in Brechtian epic theater, the audience as well as the poet is supposed to think, instead of passively receiving picturesque descriptions. So the book shifts from one kind of writing to another, from one persona to another, from one author to another, with the abruptness of fantasies or dreams. And, as Auden makes clear, the journey to Iceland would not have taken place without the elaborate saga-fantasies that had been so important to his boyhood.

Furthermore, there is considerable reference to dreams, nightmares, riddles, séances. One poem asks: "O who can paint the vivid tree/And grass of phantasy?" (*CP*, 226) Auden, of course, tries to do so and cares much less about painting the actual tree and grass of Iceland. The Auden who had used Norse imagery in England turns, in Iceland, to fantasy, fairy tale, detective story, and Lord Byron; and the connections of this travel book are as whimsical as the connections of dreams—except that everything fantastic points to the actual, everything in Iceland relates to Europe, and the very letter form suggests that the meaning of the experience is not complete until it is sent back home.

Continuous narration is, of course, impossible for Auden. Always hostile to realism, he prefers notions of gratuitous grace, sudden confrontations not earned but granted. For sequence and significance have little correlation; in remembering a trip (to Iceland, for example), we do not recall the events in chronological order but jump from one high point to another, exhibiting what Auden later praised Byron for capturing: "the motion of life." (*DH*, 405) Auden captures it here. The journey's meaning —so the structure of the book implies—is not so much in the place visited as in the rhythms of feeling, the mental connections, the insights, that the journey arouses in the travelers.

How successful is the collage? More so, I think, than most critics have been willing to say. And the book has a special interest in relation to Auden's other extended works. *Letters from Iceland* belongs to what we might call, in respect to his longer works (at least), his messy period. It begins with *The Orators* (if not with *Paid on Both Sides*) and reaches its messiest with *Dog* and *Iceland*. The other plays retreat from this extreme of untidy design, as do the longer works of the decade's end, "In Time of War" and "The Quest." But what follows then is remarkable and unexpected: first, the scrupulous couplets of "New Year Letter"; next, the careful arrangement of tableaux in *For the Time Being;* and then the spectacular craftsmanship of *The Sea and the Mirror* and *The Age of Anxiety.* In these longer works Auden has moved far from the cheerful, honest, plain disorder of *Letters from Iceland* to sophisticated artifice, from the random collage to orderly structure, from Romantic trust in whatever comes into the head to classical restraint, from Byron perhaps to Jane Austen or even to Shakespeare and Spenser. And much as we enjoy reading *Letters from Iceland,* much as we may lament the years of abstraction it cost Auden to move beyond it, we know the later work is the finer.

It appears, then, that all of Auden's excursions into casual talk either are qualified or are qualified successes. Plainness may do much, but to do all that Auden wants poetry to do, other techniques must be added: irony, obliqueness, surrealism, ambiguity. And these intimidate the audience. But plainness does not jolt enough; in fact, it may succeed best in contexts where to be plain seems odd. In a poetry where perspective matters so much, the poem's effect often depends on the relation between detail and formal context, between what the words seem to be saying and what the form implies. If the poet's *language* cannot be as simple as he would like, he may yet engage an audience by using traditional public *forms*.

CHAPTER 8

Public Forms

I *Songs and Ballads*

M ONROE SPEARS, in his book on Auden, has dealt so fully with Auden's songs (105-23) that I need not speak of them at length. Auden wrote many in the 1930's, and a number have been set to music. These songs usually achieve a simple and clean clarity of form and feeling, the quiet elegance common to the melodious tradition of Campion, Shakespeare, Jonson, Dryden, Tennyson, and Housman, all of whom Auden sometimes echoes. In these "art songs" (as distinguished from his ballads, which Spears calls "popular songs"), the poet may at times be ironic, but the irony is veiled by a certain blandness, an evenness of texture, which makes them more suitable for setting but which also encourages readers or listeners to tune out the meaning. The gist tends to escape through the multiple abstractions:

> Bells that toll across the meadows
> From the sombre spire
> Toll for these unloving shadows
> Love does not require.
> All that lives may love; why longer
> Bow to loss
> With arms across?
> Strike and you shall conquer. (*CP*, 232-33)

Words like "shadows" and "loss" come at crucial junctures where we hope for concrete words to fix meaning clearly.

From the point of view of Auden's search for generality, the songs are important. For the song is a public form; to write a song is to write for the public. Even if the songs are art songs, they are still something to sing; and vast numbers of people like to sing or to hear new songs. If the songs have good tunes, people may learn the words before they understand them, as a child learns hymns. Even without tunes at all, if the verse is rhythmic, insistent, or suggests certain attractive moods, lines of the song may sink into the mind before it quite sees what they mean. After the song is familiar, the very fact that one knows it, that its lines keep haunting one, gives it a special value, a kind of sacredness of its own; and the sacredness may be extended in part or entirely to the ideas expressed in the song. Thus the song achieves its purposes mainly through nonverbal means, through its hypnotic musical properties. And to these anyone may be susceptible.

Auden's ballads are, of course, different. There may be something of charm and hypnotic power in repeated rhythms or in certain verse formulas, but the strength of the ballad is usually in its ironies of statement or situation. And there is a kind of hovering irony in the ballad form that perhaps derives from its having been traditionally used to celebrate the ironic disproportion between public event and private feeling. The ballad strikes an immediate note of community among all those who are aware, perhaps without saying so, that the public world is not what one could wish it to be.

To be sure, the modern popular song—a "ballad" in Spears' classification—often says nothing about the public world but, by allowing the private world to become all that there is, makes a point. Thus Auden frequently parodies the phrases and attitudes of popular love songs: "He was my North, my South, my East and West,/My working week and my Sunday rest." (*CP*, 229)/"O but he was as fair as a garden in flower,/As slender and tall as the great Eiffel Tower. . . ." (*CP*, 221) But the parody is not unsympathetic. Such elegies, for all their extravagance, are moving expressions of how it feels to lose a lover. Auden's treatment shows that the extravagance of the modern popular song, if pursued with tact, can be made to yield very delicate effects.

But his more usual ballad makes a social protest and, instead of exaggerating, proceeds by understatement. Typically, his ballads show us victims of social injustice or of psychological warping. In spite of ellipsis, the situations and their significance are almost always clear. Most of them present ghastly situations— the horror of the modern world—through ordinary language, ordinary tones of voice, and ordinary imagery, so that what is principally conveyed is the impact of an impersonal society or of lunatic public policy (and the madmen who direct it) on the private life. For example, the song of the soldiers in *On the Frontier*: "The biscuits are hard and the beef is high,/The weather is wet and the drinks are dry,/We sit in the mud and wonder why." (172) Or, from the best of the poems in this vein, "Roman Wall Blues": "Over the heather the wet wind blows,/I've lice in my tunic and a cold in my nose." (*CP*, 221) Auden catches well in such songs the attempt of ordinary people to keep their lives intact in the face of the horrifying facts of military or industrial impersonality. Other ballads use similar techniques to attack totalitarian barbarism. Several narrative ballads ("Miss Gee," "Victor," "James Honeyman") show representative lost souls produced by modern society.

The most remarkable ballad of all, "As I walked out one evening," which has been analyzed extensively,[1] shows Auden so complete a master of the ballad style that he boldly exceeds its usual limits by interweaving moral generalizations with the ordinary imagery in a way that the traditional ballad does not dare to do: "The glacier knocks in the cupboard,/The desert sighs in the bed,/And the crack in the tea-cup opens/A lane to the land of the dead." (*CP*, 198) Puzzling connections and abstract imagery help to convey Auden's main perception in this poem—that the Romantic habit of expecting too much of life makes disappointment and despair likely. Ballads are usually not asked to say so much. But Auden's intensity of phrase, aptness of detail, and mastery of the ballad feeling succeed in pushing back the normal limits of the form.

And perhaps it is not merely the union of abstract and concrete that accounts for the strange force of this poem. The personification of Time and Justice, the supernatural effect of Time's speech, the odd fairy-tale archetypes (Jack and Jill, the Giant), and even the quasi-religious imperatives and confrontations ("Stare, stare . . . look, look . . . stand, stand . . .") add to the already public form of the ballad the still more extensive generalizing powers of myth.

II *Myth*

Myth, in fact, seems an inevitable resource for a poet who wishes to reach a wider audience, especially when Eliot and

Pound had made such significant use of myths in their work.
Auden's early imagery, as we have seen, amounts to a developed
mythology. It is tempting, therefore . . . But what about Romantic vagueness? That is the danger, and the poet must be
careful. By trying to say too much, he risks saying nothing distinct.

During the middle 1930's, to avoid this danger, Auden stayed
as close as he could either to plain speaking or to highly stylized
forms in which the significance of each element tended to be
quite clear. In *The Dog Beneath the Skin,* for example, the fairy-
tale plot might encourage us to feel a loose identification with
the hero; but the banal language and the hero's lack of innerness
make any such identification unrewarding. *The Ascent of F6*
plays more dangerously both with myth and with Romantic
identification: Ransom is an attractive hero, and his quest is
epical. But the playwrights' attitude is severely antiheroic: the
hero is tainted, his enterprise corrupt, and the need that Mr. and
Mrs. A. feel for public heroes is part of their illness. One of the
play's shortcomings is exactly this: that it fails to make us feel
antiheroic, fails to make us want to solve our own problems,
personal or national, in their own contexts, without recourse to
futile dreams of ourselves or others as heroes.

But with his interest in the unconscious, Auden cannot entirely
eschew the mythical. The myth of the hero may be harmful, but
all myths are not so, and art may sometimes make good use of
folk material. The songs and ballads exploit hypnotic effects or
unstated assumptions. The open, casual style, too, is often, even
typically, haunted by dreams, nightmares, the unconscious. In
many of Auden's more rhetorical, high-style poems of the 1930's,
especially in conjunction with his hawk's-eye imagery, there is
an incantatory quality that has something of the grand, priestly
air he dislikes in Milton and in the Romantics.[2] One thinks of the
pageant of Yesterdays, Todays, and Tomorrows in *Spain,* or this,
from a poem of 1933:

> Some possible dream, long coiled in the ammonite's slumber
> Is uncurling, prepared to lay on our talk and reflection
> Its military silence, its surgeon's idea of pain;
>
> And out of the future into actual history,
> As when *Merlin,* tamer of horses, and his lords to whom
> *Stonehenge* was still a thought, the *Pillars* passed

And into the undared ocean swung north their prow,
Drives throught the night and star-concealing dawn
For the virgin roadsteads of our hearts an unwavering
keel. (*CP*, 90)

If prophecy, nightmare, and balladry all use tones we know and
feelings we have but are not always aware of, the same is true of
fairy tales. During the 1930's Auden used fairy-tale structure
and motifs most extensively in *The Dog Beneath the Skin;* and
in such songs as "Now the leaves are falling fast" and " 'O for
doors to be open,' " the imagery is drawn from childish proverbs
or situations. Auden's fuller use of fairy tales came during the
1940's, when the fables and imperatives of fairy-tale lore seemed
especially appropriate to his exploration of Kierkegaardian Christianity. In *The Age of Anxiety* (1947) and in the libretto for *The
Rake's Progress* (1951), we can see later, sophisticated uses of
fairy-tale atmospheres and situations.

But there were several long works at the end of this period in
which Auden pursued further his interest in myths. His sonnet
sequence, "The Quest" (1940), uses a theme that, as he himself
says, "occurs in fairy tales, legends like The Golden Fleece and
The Holy Grail, boys' adventure stories and detective novels."[3]
Indeed, the quest motif is a permanent one in Auden's work—
understandably so, for it offers not a random series of loose
symbols but a symbolic structure in which every detail may have
a precise signification.

A second ambitious work of this time, the libretto for Benjamin
Britten's opera *Paul Bunyan* (presented at Columbia University
but never again performed or published) is also based on a
popular myth. And *The Dark Valley,* a one-act radio play commissioned by the Columbia Broadcasting Company and produced on June 2, 1940, is full of what seems like highly Romantic
symbolism. Although printed in prose, much of it is actually in
four-stress alliterative verse reminiscent of Auden's early poems
and anticipating *The Age of Anxiety* (the line-divisions are
mine): "The gold was gone; they got nothing;/they lost heart,
gave up their drilling;/it paid no longer; they departed poor./
And none remained but mother and I [*sic*]/on this stony farm
in a stony silence./She never loved me. I knew it from the first./
She was prim and pious and praying always/for father's soul

and shuddered at his songs/and thought him wicked and wept much."[4]

The play concerns an old woman almost totally isolated in a dark valley, her only companion a goose whom she now, without regret, is making plans to kill, and to whom she talks about her own past, about the wretched world, and about their meager future. Mythical overtones abound: the golden age has passed; the old woman's powerful, miracle-performing father is dead. Her mother represents conventional society; the old woman is both an observer of the modern world and that world itself. The goose, perhaps, is life; in killing it, the woman destroys herself.

To go further, the situation of the old woman, impelled to kill the goose ("I'm sorry, but it has to be done"), gruesomely parodies that of Abraham sacrificing Isaac. Auden seems to be suggesting that, in the darkness of the contemporary world, Kierkegaardian despair and resignation may be appropriate; but there is no indication at the play's end that the God who halted Abraham's sacrifice will intervene to save this old woman from a violence that will involve her own destruction.

The Dark Valley, with its bizarre image of the world's self-destruction, indicates the direction of Auden's concerns at the end of the decade. It may be said very generally that his early work through *The Orators* focuses on England; that for the next few years, perhaps through 1937, his poems and plays and his first travel book *Letters from Iceland* take Europe for their subject; but that from 1938 on, and rather grandly from 1938 to 1941, his subject is Man. This interest does not start overnight, but by 1938 the enlargement of perspective is clear and pervasive. His visit to China may have helped to widen his view. But, under the stress of the frightening events of Europe, he is rethinking his positions in the light of extensive reading in sociology, anthropology, and even theology. His interest in myth, therefore, reflects his wish to write about the nature of man in general.

But most of his work of this period *discusses* man and makes little effort to involve the general reader. It thus avoids Romantic reliance on the unconscious, whereas myth is a little suspect and, except in some secondary role, is rarely used by the later, more scrupulous Auden. The issues are subtle here: for Auden the seductive, hypnotic virtues of sound and form are perfectly acceptable in poetry; but art as magic, as propaganda, is not. Anything that draws the reader in is fair means; but it is foul to trick him into assenting to propositions, as an unrestrained symbolic art may do. Hence his gingerly use, from now on, of myth and symbol, and his feeling that the poet has the right to make his patterns of meaning cryptic but not vague. Symbols must designate, not merely suggest. Largeness is still his aim, and public forms may still help him achieve it; but after 1940 no loose emotion, no idle incantation, is tolerable. All symbolic detail must be submitted to classical design.

CHAPTER 9

The Life of Man

"WHAT IS MAN?" had by 1938 become the fundamental question for Auden, and his work for the next few years keeps trying to work out an answer. His early studies in Freudian psychology and his continued curiosity about how animals differ from human beings reflect his permanent wish to describe the species Man. But his early psychological perspective had, since about 1930, been dominated by a social perspective: man is sick, but he is sick in groups, sick largely *because* of his groups. Hence it is social problems that in this period first take up Auden's attention: how can social institutions be organized so that man need no longer be ill? Education, politics, government, the press—these are the subjects that for a while engross him.

His view is thus that of the liberal humanist, wanting to remake society so that people can be happier in it. The events of the 1930's, however, were enough to shake any man's faith in human ability to improve the world: the men who seemed to have most power to change it were rapidly making it worse. Perhaps, then, Auden's position was basically at fault. It seemed so simple a process, to examine social institutions and to improve them. But human societies do not work that way, not just because this or that institution resists reform, but because man is deeper than his institutions.

Auden's contribution to *Journey to a War* (1939) is the first large work that exhibits this perspective and the style that goes with it, neither of them entirely new but both now newly dominant. *Letters from Iceland* having proved moderately successful, Auden was commissioned with Isherwood to travel to China and to report on the war then in progress against the invading Japanese. *Journey to a War*, the result, is dominated by Isherwood's extended account of their journey from Hong Kong to the interior and eventually to Shanghai, a prose report characterized by Isherwood's usual narrative expertness—amusing, absorbing, and wonderfully clear. Auden's contribution—diminished in this second travel book as it was in the later plays—consists of the dedicatory sonnet to E. M. Forster, a short poem, "The Voyage," and five sonnets, all of which precede Isherwood's long narrative, and "In Time of War," which comes after and comprises a sonnet sequence and a verse commentary.

The introductory sonnets, several of which reflect on the meaning of journeys in general, get us by stages to China. Since Isherwood's prose takes care of their activities *in* China, the sonnet sequence and its verse commentary show us the *meaning* of their journey. "In Time of War" actually tries to do more: its highly abstract and impersonal sonnets formulate the nature of man—troubled, weak, yet capable of love and free to choose it. The opening sonnets survey human history, each from a different point of view, so that the history is not at all continuous; each angle of vision is independent of the others and allows us to see only a part of the total picture. There is even a sort of Jamesian technique at work here: in each sonnet we see what the subject sees (the poet, the peasant, etc.); and we also see that which can be seen by looking at him, by taking him for the moment as the center of things.

The same shifting technique continues throughout the sequence, but the more omniscient sonnets, XII and XIII, make a bridge to a group directly concerned with the Chinese War. Again each one studies a different aspect of the war—the planes, the Japanese pilots, the soldiers planning, wounded or dead—and its meaning. Then gradually the sonnets become more general ("The life of man is never quite completed"—XXI), and Auden leaves China to comment even more abstractly on the nature of human history: "We have no destiny assigned us . . . we are articled to error . . . We live in freedom by necessity. . . ." (XXV, XXVII)

That self-inclusive "we" does not obscure the fundamental detachment of the speaker. In earlier volumes Auden's diagnosis of the significance of gestures, habits, diseases, and actions had usually been supported by a vividly sketched landscape or by a warmly casual tone; but here the tone and imagery have become remote and strained. The observer is no longer a full person but an objective commentator, a stylish surgeon dispassionately feeling out the malignant lump: "Wandering lost upon the mountains of our choice,/Again and again we sigh for an ancient South. . . ." (XXVII) The mountains are symbolic, not actual; so is the South; all the situations are generalized; and objects, persons, and places seem useful to the speaker only as illustrations. But the abstraction does give the verse an impressive dignity and implies that the situation is now so appalling that mere vividness would be trivial. The Rilkean style intensifies the detachment of the sonnets; the unspecified perspectives and unlocated third-person pronouns make each sonnet partly a riddle and encourage the reader to go through the same figuring-out process that the poet is himself engaged in.

The metallic tonelessness of these sonnets approximates that of some war correspondents' reports—taut, tense, tough, like a more intellectual and abstract Hemingway in the avoidance of obvious emotion, the eye for the revealing detail, the unsmiling amusement at passing ironies. Indeed, this detail and these ironies, though always quietly observed, seem to burst out, like sudden shots in a quiet place, from the general abstraction. Usually these bursts occur when the poet sees something in a new way: "A telephone is speaking to a man . . ." (XVI); or, of the wounded: "A bandage hides the place where each is living. . . ." (XVII)

Lines like these dispassionately call attention to the divergence between what one can observe and what is actually happening. Muted similes often compare things of different dimensions: "Here war is simple like a monument . . ." (XVI) or "The cities hold his feeling like a fan;/And crowds make room for him without a murmur,/As the earth has patience with the life of man." (*CP*, 55) Often, external things are likened to internal or intellectual ones. The attacking Japanese airplanes, for example, "take us by surprise/Like ugly long-forgotten memories,/And like a conscience all the guns resist." (XIV) In the hospital the wounded "lie apart like epochs from each other." (XVII)

Indeed, the whole poem draws together the world of external event, the world of inner event, and the conceptual world, by exposing their mutual alienation. And alienation is the major theme here. The poem works in smaller syntactical units than Auden ordinarily uses: as the above quotations suggest, he aims at the effective single line. Even the tercets and quatrains seem curt, on guard. Connections between events are consecutive, not causal; the poems are full of *and*'s, which isolate events and actions, and of *the*'s, which isolate things and people. Each sonnet is detached and separate; they, too, "lie apart like epochs from each other." It seems likely that Auden meant his poem to be like the war he is reporting—direct, impersonal, measured, yet capable of sporadic human outbursts.

The Commentary (a dozen pages of unrhymed iambic triplets, varying from five to eight stresses but so conversational in rhythm that we may easily ignore the iambic beat) explains more straightforwardly, and in more extended periods, the significance, in the whole history of mankind, of the Chinese war, for it "Is but the local variant of a struggle in which all/ . . . In all their living are profoundly implicated." (*CP*, 338-39) Using much variation and corroborative imagery, Auden names the enemies of this struggle: "All the great conquerors" and such other assorted villains as Plato, Macchiavelli, Hobbes, and Hegel. But still, the poet goes on, we also have our leaders who tell us how to build "*a world united.*" It may yet be possible to "*construct at last a human justice.*"[1]

Some of the Commentary is stiff and prosy. Of goodness he says: ". . . even to exist, it must be shared as truth,/ As freedom or as happiness. (For what is happiness/If not to witness joy upon the features of another?)" (*CP*, 344) Some of it is deadly quiet, as in mechanical iambs it speaks of mechanical horror:

> Now in a world that has no localized events,
> Where not a tribe exists without its dossier,
> And the machine has taught us how, to the Non-Human,
>
> That unprogressive blind society that knows
> No argument except the absolute and violent veto,
> Our colours, creeds and sexes are identical,
>
> The issue is the same. (*CP*, 339-40)

At other moments the verse is very grand, in the hawk's-eye manner:

> Night falls on China; the great arc of travelling shadow

> Moves over land and ocean, altering life:
> Thibet already silent, the packed Indias cooling,
>
> Inert in the paralysis of caste. And though in Africa
>   . . . (*CP*, 346)

This passage, which extends its sublime imagery for another seventeen lines, shows the broadness of Auden's perspective. Beyond the constrictions of tone, the occasional prosiness, the dryness everywhere, he tries to lead us to this large view of man. It is still a humanist view, a view of man in society. But now, as it broadens, it withdraws not only from the immediacies of England and Europe but from those of the sensory world itself. If, for Auden, the fundamental realities had always been hidden from view, the outer symptoms had at least been fascinating, and fun to depict and to interpret. But now the situation is too grim. The diseases and weaknesses which through the early poetry could have their charming and attractive aspects have now turned into unambiguous horrors; the life to avoid is not merely that of pleasant self-indulgence but the ghastly Death-in-Life of the machine:

> "*Man can have Unity if Man will give up Freedom.*
>
> *The State is real, the Individual is wicked;*
> *Violence shall synchronize your movements like a tune,*
> *And Terror like a frost shall halt the flood of thinking.*" (*CP*, 342)

Thus, as beneath the telephone's apparent action and the bandage's concealment something desperate is really happening, Auden tries to discern the hidden currents operating within man and within civilizations, forces that have brought mankind to its present appalling predicament. In the poet's search for the large patterns underlying modern history, he almost forgets for a while the visible world, or he uses it only as a source of illustrations or of points of departure for his large statements. That this practice, in a sense, reinforces the life-draining powers that he detests is one of the ironies of this period for Auden; but it appears that he could not rest in his confusion, he *had* to live among abstractions for a time—even if this meant temporarily abandoning clarity and the possibly wide audience—in order to find his way back to the actual world again.[2]

CHAPTER 10

Toward Agape

I *Eros, Logos, Kairos, Agape*

A T THE END of the 1930's Auden slowly makes his intellectual way from liberal humanism to Kierkegaardian Christianity. Ironically, as he deplores the mechanization of modern society, his own poems become more removed from ordinary sensuous existence. Cities and great men, parading before him, submit to his examination; but too often the life they must once have possessed is reduced to an idea. If many such poems have a fineness of intellectual outline, we still miss the warmth of his more personal poems: this enlarged perspective treats even inwardness from outside. Convinced of the value of the instinctive life, but distrusting such wayward manifestations of the irrational as Nazism, the increasingly rationalist Auden detaches himself from his subject: inwardness is not a sea to dream in and drown in, but a realm of existence whose laws the intelligent man must seek to understand without distortion or destruction.

Gradually, in this period, as we can see in Auden's reviews and articles, his political militancy declines: the Marxism withers; the faith in social democracy, which in December, 1938, is to be defended, "if necessary, at the cost of our lives,"[1] is no longer sufficient a year later when the war has broken out: "When the ship catches fire, it seems only natural to rush importantly to the pumps, but perhaps one is only adding to the general confusion and panic: to sit still and pray seems selfish and unheroic, but it may be the wisest and most helpful course."[2]

Early in 1939 Auden could sympathize with Voltaire's view of the Catholic Church as one of the "three great enemies" of democracy and freedom.[3] But as the year proceeds, he begins to bring into his reviews such terms as "mortal sins," "damnation," "pride," "repentance," "faith." Economic solutions are not enough:

"there is not the slightest reason to suppose that owning the means of production will create for the people a sudden traditional source of value."[4]

For, granted the unconscious is a dangerous guide, we still cannot count on man to be reasonable. Besides, while his social organization ought to be rationally arranged, the irrational remains the source of much that is important and valuable. What we must do is not to oppose these forces against each other, but to use them both, to recognize that both work together to produce the whole man.[5] As Auden discusses these matters, theological terms soon replace the secular ones. He had long used Eros in Freud's sense to mean Love or the forces of life. Now it becomes a term for the purely irrational, the disordered energy of uncontrolled life, even the rather lunatic Id. And opposed to Eros is Logos, the form, the outline, which gives shape, meaning, order, to the random force of Eros. Eros is admirable insofar as it represents honest feeling, love, "the basic will to self-actualization without which no creature can exist."[6] But too often it is perverted and becomes a destructive force. Such destruction can be prevented by order and reason, especially with the aid of science, whose method is still "the only way of asking questions to obtain valid knowledge."[7] This order is not, therefore, the kind that tyrannizes, against which Auden is always strong, but the kind that liberates for constructive activity, the routine that allows work to get done, the method that makes for progress.

In actual life, order (the human expression of the divine Logos) tends to be provided by attention to the immediate, to the present moment and its concerns, to whatever is before one or whatever activity the moment seems best fitted for. The Greeks had a word, "Kairos," for this moment—"the propitious moment for doing something" (*DH*, 140n.)—and it is one of Auden's favorite terms in these years. Thus, although in one sense Logos (as form and order) is opposed to Eros (force and energy), from another point of view Logos (as eternal) is opposed to Kairos (the immediate moment), or, rather, distinct from it. For, between Logos and Kairos, eternal law and immediate moment, there is a metaphysical but not an ethical distinction. We reach Logos through Kairos.

Eros, on the other hand, is dangerous. In fact, the history of

Western Europe is dominated by two equally treacherous here-
sies—"isotypes of Eros"—each of which is, of course, best summed
up in parabolical figures: Tristan and Don Giovanni. The Tristan
myth derives from "Manicheism, a dualistic heresy introduced
into Europe from the East, which held matter to be the creation
of the Evil One and therefore incapable of salvation. From this
it follows that all human institutions like marriage are corrupt,
and perfection can be reached only by death, in which the limitations of matter are finally transcended and the soul is merged
into the infinite nothingness of the Logos."[8]

For Tristan and Iseult love is predestined, they have no responsibility for it, and it "can exist in the world of time only so long
as there are obstacles to its physical consummation; only after
death can they be at last eternally identified in the Infinite."
(756) In Don Giovanni, on the other hand, "it is the flesh that
is asserted and the spirit that is denied; the present moment is
all, the eternal future nothing. Tristan sees time as something
evil to be passively endured; Don Juan sees time as something
evil to be aggressively destroyed: the former is a suicide, the
latter a murderer." (757)

Unlike animals, who live only among actualities, human beings
live amid the actual and the possible. But Don Giovanni's actual
is undermined by his sense of the possibilities (all the women
who are not yet on his list), and Tristan's "myth of passion . . .
that is, that only perfection is worthy to be loved," is undermined
when the actual "physical world invades and destroys his consciousness." (757) What each man needs to do is to accept the
fact that every moment limits the formerly infinite number of
possibilities, to have faith in his choices even though he knows
that he may have chosen wrongly.

If these two myths show the wrong kinds of love, the right
kind is Agape, which is "Eros mutated by Grace, a conversion,
not an addition." (757) The Divine Love, which breathes life
into form, makes the Word incarnate in the Flesh, reconciles
Eros and Logos. For ordinary human beings in a society that
has been gradually split into smaller and smaller units where
real community is difficult, where "men no longer have neighbors tied to them by geography, only a far-flung association of
personal friends kept in touch with by machinery,"[9] the problem
is somehow "to seek *Agape* in the everyday world,"[10] not in an

other-worldly abstraction and asceticism. For Auden, in his Christian phase just as in his earlier work, one of the worst human offenses is to hide, to fail to deal with the facts—the outer world of social corruption, the inner world of anxiety, guilt, and love. Hence, while we must be aware of the eternal, the setting for action and choice is here and now. And only Agape can reconcile eternity and time, the Love to Whom Auden appeals in the poem, "Kairos and Logos," to help the world: "O Thou who lovest, set its love in order." (*CP*, 12)

II *The Leap of Faith*

We might expect an inveterate rationalist like Auden to pause on the edge of so mystical a faith. It did take him several years to accept it, as he relates in his contribution to *Modern Canterbury Pilgrims*.[11] According to this report, the progress of Auden's conversion was far less intellectual than his reviews of the time suggest. After a childhood of close familiarity with church services and the Bible, he proceeded to the liberal humanism which seemed the only sensible outlook for "civilized people." The Communist attack on Christianity encouraged him to be anti-Christian, but the Nazi attack on it made him think again.

In this state of mind he found, on his visit to Spain, that churches meant something to him, after all; he met Charles Williams "and for the first time in my life felt myself in the presence of personal sanctity" (41); and as he began to read Kierkegaard and other theological works, "I was forced to know in person what it is like to feel oneself the prey of demonic powers, in both the Greek and the Christian sense, stripped of self-control and self-respect, behaving like a ham actor in a Strindberg play." (41) By the autumn of 1940 he had taken the leap of faith and become a Christian.

It is clear enough what attractions Christianity possessed for a man of Auden's temperament. Where liberal humanism insisted that the conditions of life must inevitably improve, although anyone in the late 1930's could see them getting worse and worse, Christian faith, with its longer perspective, could interpret present reverses as part of a more complex pattern. Christianity could thus provide what was indispensable to Auden: a ground of acceptance of the world in all its apparent evil. It could also shift the ground of acceptance from such a shaky future as, in his occasional utopian visions, Auden had never been at ease with—to the present moment seen in the light of eternity. Thus the Christian perspective opened two doors of hope, one metaphysical, one ethical: first, if the world seemed nasty now, it could yet be good in the long run; second, no matter how depressing its nastiness, a man's business was not to judge it (God would do that) or to wish to change it miraculously (the Romantics had wished that) but to work quietly at his own limited tasks.

Furthermore, the Christian view of reality fitted perfectly Auden's symbolic (or allegorical) habits of thought. From his earliest work the phenomenal world had served him principally as a reservoir of symbols. He never denies its actuality and often insists on it, but he insists also on seeing beneath its surfaces, on subjecting it to different perspectives which have the effect of showing it always to be not quite what we had thought. In a sense, Auden, whose way of thinking seems at times remarkably Platonic, has always aimed at finding the right underlying pattern, the magic formula, that would validate the actual world. If in the late 1930's his poetry seems to lose touch with that world, it is because for him existence without meaning is a contradiction in terms; and the meanings that had been warming his world were turning cold. Christianity renews them, gives them life.

Perhaps most congenial to Auden in the Christian framework are certain basic patterns on which he has since laid great stress. As in his poetry the chief characteristic is surprise, its chief technique the sudden dislocation of perspective, so his theology emphasizes the unexpected. Of the finite universe whose conditions are mainly knowable by reason, God is the unconditional creator. And, as He is beyond conditions, so is one's choice of Him. One believes not because one is convinced, nor in hope of being convinced, but in despair and resignation. And then, as with Abraham, as with the fairy-tale hero (a third son, like Auden) who in defeat gives away his last coin to the beggar woman, the miracle occurs and one gets everything back—the world, light, hope, meaning. Not of one's own doing, nor even of one's own deserving, for Agape is a gift not earned but conferred by Grace.

94

It is all very Kierkegaardian; Auden's Protestantism is profoundly influenced by the Danish philosopher and borrows his insights, distinctions, terms. For both men are interested in the rational analysis, from a Christian point of view, of an inner life driven by a logic all its own. Auden refers especially often to Kierkegaard's division of perspectives into the Aesthetic, the Ethical, and the Religious; and he frequently explains and extends this classification, which he finds most useful for proving that the only acceptable view of life is the one he has chosen. The Aesthetic attitude (or even religion) honors passionate existence; its divinity (epitomized in the Greek gods of Homer)—what it regards as the source of human effectiveness—is identified with external and unpredictable powers (luck), who impose their will from outside the human being. The Ethical attitude honors knowledge, reason; its divinity (epitomized in the God of Greek philosophy) is the knowledge of good and evil. The weakness of both attitudes is, in effect, that nothing guarantees existence when no one is there, when passion or the Greek gods absent themselves or when reason is asleep.

But existence, one's relation to the ground of being, cannot be intermittent; and one must therefore find a more reliable ground —something which is essentially outside consciousness and therefore more objective than passion or reason: God. "God is not present as an object of consciousness. . . . God is not knowable as an object."[12] The Christian God for Auden is something to which one cannot *not* be related: "there is only a question of the right relation."[13] And the right relation quite neatly synthesizes the Necessity of the Aesthetic and the Freedom of the Ethical views: "The commands of God are neither the aesthetic fiat, 'Do what you must' nor the ethical instruction, "These are the things which you may or must not do,' but the call of duty, 'Choose to do what at this moment in this context I am telling you to do.' "[14]

The Aesthetic and the Ethical are not precisely congruent with Auden's early terms, the "Unconscious" and "Reason," nor certainly with "Eros" and "Logos"; but his readers ought to be aware of a certain continuity in the patterns of these favorite oppositions. Kierkegaard supplies Auden with what his thought has hitherto lacked—a synthesizing third term (the Religious category, and Agape[15]) which satisfactorily resolves the opposi-

tion between the other two. Now, with a standard of value outside the private psychological life, and coming from beyond
either reason or feeling, a poet ought to be able to make poems
that are neither too Romantic nor too abstract but that reproduce
in their form the patterns that exist in the world—specifically,
the pattern in which such opposed polarities as reason and
feeling do not struggle for mastery but give to man what they
have to give, in the service of an enabling higher source. All his
later work will try to realize this situation.

The value of this work does not exactly depend on the validity
of the poet's religious beliefs, but his portrait of life owes much
to his view of its sources. Without convictions, without a philo-
sophic framework of belief, his craft suffers: "Art is not metaphysics any more than it is conduct, and the artist is usually
unwise to insist too directly in his art upon his beliefs; but without an adequate and conscious metaphysics in the background,
art's imitation of life inevitably becomes, either a photostatic
copy of the accidental details of life without pattern or significance, or a personal allegory of the artist's individual dementia,
of interest primarily to the psychologist and the historian."[16]

From the point of view of his art, Auden's devotion to abstraction during these years was necessary to the elaboration of an
intellectual structure that could serve as the basis for all his
subsequent work. If, in the later 1930's, his poetry went consistently in the direction of greater generality, it was only
through his developed framework of ideas that he came to write
at last with this generality beneath him, assumed, a part of
every poem, so pervasively present that he could in time return
to the personal and give it genuine largeness.

CHAPTER 11

Down Among the Lost People

I Another Time: *Chronology*

FOR ANYONE who wants to understand Auden's development as a poet, his third main collection *Another Time* (1940) is a confusing and miscellaneous volume—inevitably so, when we consider how fast his ideas were changing and how variously he was trying to achieve largeness without Romantic sublimity. If his early work takes its character from Nordic imagery and the elliptical manner, and if *On This Island* is dominated by a developing musical verve and elegance, *Another Time* seems marked by its abstraction, by the poet's disposition to discuss, to comment on, and to fix the value of, men, cities, civilizations, events, aspects of life.

But the fifty poems of this book are very diverse in their styles, and Auden's arrangement of them seems calculated (as in his collections of the next decade) to disguise the current of his thinking: the reader is invited to take each poem as a poem, not as a chapter in the personal history of the poet. Still, it is just this development, the unity in his diversity, that his critics have usually misread. And since Auden himself in his poems (especially those in this volume) and reviews has often followed the changes in other eminent men, his objection is to the poet's stressing his own development, not to the critic's piecing it together. For most scholars, understanding a poem involves seeing it in relation to other poems by the same poet.

The poems of *Another Time*, therefore, can be read in two ways: first, as Auden has arranged them, in three groups divided on a basis that, though rough, is formal. The book opens with a long section of thirty-one poems ("People and Places"); continues with a second section ("Lighter Poems") of eight parts, which in fact include thirteen poems (mainly songs and ballads); and concludes with a third section ("Occasional Poems") made up of six more ambitious poems—five elegies (the poems on Spain, Yeats, Freud, and Ernst Toller, and "September 1, 1939") and one epithalamion. A plausible and even helpful division, it obscures Auden's development in this period; and in some ways the volume becomes more coherent if we see it as composed of chronological and stylistic layers, if we look at it not logically, as a democracy of forms, but historically, as a succession of dynasties.

Thus, to begin with, most of the songs and ballads of the second section, and some other poems as well, are, in a sense, left over from the energetic musical period of the middle 1930's: "Orpheus," "Danse Macabre," "Lay your sleeping head," "O lurcher-loving collier" (from a movie Auden worked on in 1935), "O the valley in the summer," "Stop all the clocks" (from *The Ascent of F6*), "Miss Gee," "Victor," and "Wrapped in a yielding air." These poems share many qualities with the poems in *On This Island*: the elegant polished expression of longing, the deliberate flatness of colloquial language used to heighten the ballad's impersonal pathos, and celebration in song of the differences between man and the rest of the universe. All these poems appear to have been written no later than 1937.

By 1937, however, the more discursive of Auden's poems begin to show signs of fatigue. His visit to Spain from January to March no doubt had much to do with the change. I have already suggested that *Spain* rings false, that the verse in the later plays loses its life, and that Auden's contributions to "In Time of War" are strong, but in a tight, tense way. The same quiet constriction is to be noted in almost all the poems Auden wrote in 1937 and 1938 and perhaps some of the 1939 ones as well: "Dover," "Schoolchildren," "Oxford," "Brussels in Winter," "The Capital," "Rimbaud," "The Novelist," "The Composer," "Gare du Midi," "A. E. Housman."

Effective as some of these poems are—they all have a certain force—they share a bleakness of outlook. The speaker in all of them describes, formulates, interprets; but he never steps into the life he peers at. The streets, the railway stations, the restaurants of the modern world become the focus of an intellectual despair:

> In unlighted streets you hide away the appalling;
> Factories where lives are made for a temporary use
> Like collars or chairs, rooms where the lonely are
> > battered
> Slowly like pebbles into fortuitous shapes. (*CP*, 100)

> The improper word
> Scribbled upon the fountain, is that all the rebellion?
> (*CP*, 53)

The quiet irony, the defeated tone, the sense of pervasive horror evenly noted, justify our thinking of these poems, along perhaps with "In Time of War," as Auden's Inferno; and the comparison with Dante, whom Auden soon after this period in "New Year Letter" considered his chief mentor, might well be pursued further.[1]

Then early in 1939 Auden moved to the United States, and we can see almost at once a resurgence of spirit. Perhaps it begins before his emigration, with the relaxed and affirmative "Musée des Beaux Arts," a product of his sojourn in Brussels in late 1938. Along with his reading in sociology, history, and anthropology, he has begun to look at works on theology, especially at Kierkegaard and at Charles Williams' masterly account of the history of Christianity, *The Descent of the Dove*. From the impasse of the contemporary world—the defeat of Spain, the increasing power of Hitler, the hypocrisy of England and France —Christianity seems to offer a way out, at first doubtful and improbable; by mid-1939 conceivable if mistaken; then admissible at least as a hypothesis; and at last, sometime in 1940, accepted as the truth.

It is a disturbed but fruitful period; and the poems begin, in 1939, to shake off, little by little, the mood of despair. If "Musée des Beaux Arts" is the first of these poems to speak easily and freely again, it is followed by the impressive elegies on Yeats and Freud, by the fine ballad "Refugee Blues," the satirical "The Unknown Citizen," and the surprisingly personal "The Prophets" and "September 1, 1939." None of these poems slights the seriousness of the world situation, but some of them recover grounds for hope, affirmation, and ease. Although poetry is said in the

Yeats poem to make nothing happen in any large way (poets are not unacknowledged legislators), it can help us singly. The poet can "Still persuade us to rejoice," start "the healing fountain" in "the deserts of the heart," and "Teach the free man how to praise." (*CP*, 51) Freud, too, has helped to make us more free: "He quietly surrounds all our habits of growth;/He extends, till the tired in even/The remotest most miserable duchy/Have felt the change in their bones and are cheered. . . ." (*CP*, 166) The speaker of "September 1, 1939," though he recognizes the seriousness of the times, does so in rhythms at times almost blithe, and ends by seeking to "Show an affirming flame." (*CP*, 59)

As these poems are generally brighter in outlook, they also achieve an openness of manner, a fullness of tone (muted, of course, in the satirical pieces) that had been lacking in Auden's work since his "Letter to Lord Byron." The speaker is still a shrewd observer and acute analyst of the world around him; but now, instead of the cold formulations of the controlled scientist, we find the warmer tones, the more natural rhythms, and the more casual locutions of ordinary good conversation: "About suffering they were never wrong,/The Old Masters . . ./In Brueghel's *Icarus*, for instance: how everything turns away/ Quite leisurely from the disaster . . ." (*CP*, 3); "You were silly like us . . ." (*CP*, 50); "Perhaps I always knew what they were saying. . . ." (*CP*, 99) Even the satiric poems swing along in a relaxed way: "Say this city has ten million souls,/Some are living in mansions, some are living in holes. . . ." (*CP*, 227)

Not that all the poems of this time are relaxed and genial: these satiric poems are aimed at very somber actualities, and Auden never wrote a poem that breathes more despair than "Where do they come from," with its nightmare vision of daemonic forces within us that match (and have produced) the horrors of the contemporary world: "For the barren must wish to bear though the Spring/Punish; and the crooked that dreads to be straight/Cannot alter its prayer but summons/Out of the dark a horrible rector." (*CP*, 170) The period is a transitional one, hovering between hope and horror, yet even this poem returns to a richer imagery and more natural phrasing and rhythm (it is one of his first syllabic poems) than we find in his earlier, stiff sonnets.

II *Four Key Poems*

Auden's uncertainty during 1939 and his gradual progress from liberal humanism toward Christianity can be seen with particular clarity in one set of four poems which, though Auden separates them in *Another Time,* he may have intended to be taken together. These four are all concerned with representative thinkers (Voltaire, Arnold, Melville, and Pascal); all have essentially the same meter (regular iambic lines usually of varying lengths, usually arranged in stanzas); and the first two poems rhyme.

"Voltaire at Ferney" (first published in March, 1939) shows the secular reformer, committed to "civilise," to make society more decent, more humane, by "Cajoling, scolding, scheming." (*CP*, 6) "The night was full of wrong,/Earthquakes and executions," and he goes on struggling against them, mainly with his poetry: "Only his verses/Perhaps could stop them." Of this hope, though, Auden, who once thought poetry could "make action urgent and its nature clear" (*OTI*, XXX), has grown more skeptical; for in his Yeats elegy, published the day before the poem on Voltaire, he asserts that "poetry makes nothing happen." Voltaire is much more hopeful: he "never doubted, like D'Alembert, he would win." The poem stresses this sureness of Voltaire, his confidence in a cause that to us appears so dark. Less sanguine, its verse moving fast, Auden's poem gives us a sense of Voltaire's activity; but we see him from a distance, a gaunt, irascible old man, fighting tirelessly what seems a losing battle.[2]

"Matthew Arnold," published in September, 1939, presents another secular reformer, one more decisively defeated. Arnold is shown as having betrayed the poetry in him, which might have expressed creatively his interior "disorder." Instead, he lectured his contemporaries on their faults—a mistake, says Auden, who had not yet disencumbered his own criticism of the "jailor's voice" that he deplores in the poem. (*CP*, 54)

Indeed, the poems of 1939, as their more open style suggests, often work vaguely toward a renewed personalism of the kind Auden had entertained before his Marxist phase. Personal love teaches us much: "Bless you, darling," he can say to one lover; "I have/Found myself in you." (*CP*, 108) His "Epithalamion" suggests that the physical experience of love may symbolically

101

"justify/Life on earth." (*CP*, 173) And he praises Yeats and Freud not for their commitment to any noble social ideal—for Yeats, quite the contrary—but for what their achievement may mean for the personal life. Clearly, in this phase, though one does well to be on the right side, political and social problems have to await the resolution of inner disorder.

The last two poems of the set of four show something different—not so much resignation as actual hope. Both were published in the Autumn, 1939, *Southern Review.* "Herman Melville" concentrates not on the years of rebellion or of silence but on Melville's reconciliation with the cosmos and his approach to something like blessedness: "Towards the end he sailed into an extraordinary mildness. . . ." (*CP*, 146) He has insights into the nature of Evil and Good and realizes that "all the time he had been carried on his father's breast." The result of this final "exultation and surrender" (Melville is more like Simeon than is the Simeon of *For the Time Being*) is, of course, *Billy Budd,* in which Melville at last accepts and affirms things as they are.

The series is completed in "Pascal," which purports to describe and explain that thinker's religious history. This poem, the most triumphant of the four, appears most clearly to affirm the Christianity which, in fact, Auden had not yet come to. The triumph is, unfortunately, more religious than poetic; for the poem, though linked firmly to the three just discussed, is also the first of a series (the rest will appear in book form for the first time in 1945 in *Collected Poetry*) of highly abstract, symbolic, difficult, polished stanzaic poems in which impact is fatally sacrificed to metaphysical and formal subtlety ("Kairos and Logos," "In Sickness and in Health," and "Canzone"). It is too much to assume that Auden in "Pascal," or in "Melville," describes experiences of his own, but he is feeling his way into such inward dramas as he knows have touched the lives of other men of letters; and he is thinking about the nature and shape of the experience of conversion.

In "The Prophets" he even tries out this experience; in "New Year Letter" (1941) he goes the whole way. But, before we come to that work, we should notice one other kind of poem that appears in *Another Time.* This final group shows convincingly that the problem of abstraction in his verse is by no means shunted aside; for these poems, presumably written late in 1939,[3] are studies of such abstract themes as Hell, Law, and Time. Four in number ("Law Like Love," "Hell," "Our Bias," and "Another Time"), they are all exceedingly well turned (all of them are included in his 1958 selection); and, in spite of their abstraction, some of them have an odd warmth, even a muted joy, very different from the more usual abstraction of the late 1930's. "Law Like Love," for example, revives in a new form the old Auden playfulness:

> Law, says the judge as he looks down his nose,
> Speaking clearly and most severely,
> Law is as I've told you before,
> Law is as you know I suppose,
> Law is but let me explain it once more,
> Law is The Law. (*CP*, 75)

And the poem's conclusion, spoken to some loved person, has a disarming gentleness—the first sign of that smiling benevolence which, to the outrage of his socially conscious critics, continues to mark his work throughout its Christian phases: "If we, dear, know we know no more/Than they about the law,/If I no more than you/Know what we should and should not do. . . ."

Apparently, one solution to the problem of reconciling the abstract and the concrete is to present the ordinary man's feeling response to ideas, as the ideas are made real in the world around him. Auden has used this technique before; but from this point on, his performance is assured because of his own fuller certainty about what he is doing, about his aesthetic, about his metaphysics, and about the relationship between them.

To be sure, for a poet as much given to generalizing as Auden is, and to saying large things about man without saying large things about himself, abstraction is always a danger. Through his poems of the next few years he continues to discuss the world, often in abstract terms and often with too little of the personal voice. Still, it is clear that for Auden the nadir of his despair had come in 1938 and that in 1939, though yet uncertainly, new lights had begun to edge away the darkness. When in 1940, a year of apprehension for everyone else, Auden resolved his metaphysical dilemmas, he acquired the means by which, not all at once but in different ways here and there, he could leave his abstract Olympus (or Hades) and revisit the life to which its laws referred.

CHAPTER 12

Thing and Meaning

I *Abstraction*

BUT THE PROBLEM of abstraction requires further comment. Impersonal, detached, its imagery serving to illustrate general ideas, not to show us the abundant life of the world, the poetry of this transitional period is weak in Eros, strong in Logos. The techniques of personification and psychological landscape become automatic and careless ("the deserts of the heart," "the mountains of my fear," "the ponds of apperception"). Epigrammatist that he is, Auden can often sustain his verse for a considerable time by direct statement alone; but even when he slips into imagery, it is abstract and often quietly bizarre.

For example, the elegy on Yeats contains several images so odd, or so far extended, as to parody the metaphysical conceit:

> The provinces of his body revolted,
> The squares of his mind were empty,
> Silence invaded the suburbs,
> The current of his feeling failed . . .
>
>   *   *   *
>
> The mercury sank in the mouth of the dying day.
>
>   *   *   *
>
> The peasant river was untempted by the fashionable quays;
> By mourning tongues
> The death of the poet was kept from his poems. (*CP*, 49)

I suspect that most admirers of the poem fail to see how far its little jokes are carried. The most extended of all is the comparison of poetry to a river:

>   it survives
> In the valley of its saying where executives
> Would never want to tamper; it flows south

> From ranches of isolation and the busy griefs,
> Raw towns that we believe and die in; it survives,
> A way of happening, a mouth. (*CP,* 50)

How many readers actually see that pun on "mouth"? But it matters very much to the dignity and seriousness of the poem that we should be aware of the clowning imagery that guards against sentimentality by echoing the childish impulse to laugh at funerals, and so manages to present, more completely than it otherwise could, the whole feeling of a mourner.

But all these abstract poems do not have this emotional range. And, characteristically in Auden's work of this time, there is no poetry of objects, of sensory experience. He is *always* writing of abstract ideas, so that it almost never happens that one sensory object is compared with another. To portray the concepts, he invents landscapes; but these, instead of being developed for their own sake, function only as allegorical topographies that point back to concepts. Reality, as always for Auden, is beyond the actual; the actual is merely a parable for the real. Intrigued as he is by classifications and schemes, distinctions and categories, feeling at home with highly articulated structures of thought, he exploits whatever imageries can represent reality's most basic arrangements: war, quests, landscapes, dreams, fairy tales. These are "sacred" realms; our imaginations respond to their presence with awe. They can, therefore, in theory provide his drier abstractions with life. Although the abstraction is here more real than the thing, Logos more basic than Eros, both need each other; and they need as well to be not so much joined as fused, the Logos made incarnate through some artistic equivalent of Agape.

For a while this fusion does not happen often enough in Auden's abstract verse—not until the first impact of his theological zeal is over and the doctrines begin (in the poetry) to be assimilated to, instead of seeming to dominate and impoverish, the personal life. For if Agape has a poetic equivalent in this heavenly geometry of Auden, it is surely the sense of the man in the poem—poet, hero, or protagonist, someone whose feeling, as it changes and develops, reconciles abstraction and image.

Abstraction in itself, though dangerous for a poet, is not, however, all villain. To abstract a thing is to take it out of its context in order to have a good look at its nature. In intellectual affairs, to abstract something is, in effect, to make a separate entity of it—to make it into a thing in itself, a thing in its own right—so that we can talk about it as something independent of, or in formal relation to, all those other things among which in actual experience it is always found. Hence the personification, the hypostasizing of aspects and elements of reality, so that people, places, ideas, and forces can be spread out on the operating table like maps and their parts inspected and pointed out as if they were elements of a landscape.

This practice is an ancient one; all analyses of emotion, spirit, mental faculties (imagination, ego, feeling), proceed in this convenient fashion. So do modern physicists and chemists, as they construct models (allegories, really) to depict events they cannot see. So do myths, in their choosing to personify cosmic forces or aspects of the self. And so, in more obscure ways, do dreams and fairy tales. When Auden operates on any of these landscapes, he is expert at isolating the symbolic tissue, but much less effective at restoring its flesh and blood.

II Dinge *and Names*

The model for this abstract technique is clearly Rilke. Auden's first "Rilkean sonnet" appears in his 1928 volume, there are several in *On This Island,* but they multiply in the later 1930's when he produces more than sixty of them. Rilke, like Auden, is concerned with interior anxieties, pressures, urgencies; and, as in the following passages from the Third Duino Elegy, he fills the inner life with abstractions and personifications:

> his tall cloaked destiny stepped
> behind the chest of drawers, and his restless future
> that easily got out of place, conformed to the
> folds of the curtain.
>
> . . . .
> Descended,
> lovingly, into the older blood, the ravines
> where Frightfulness lurked, still gorged with his
> fathers. And every
> terror knew him, and winked, and quite understood.
> Yes, Horror smiled at him . . .[1]

Auden was rereading Rilke in 1939-40 and discussing him at length in reviews. In one especially illuminating passage he praises Rilke for having found "a fresh solution" to the problem of expressing "abstract ideas in concrete terms":

> . . . Rilke thinks of the human in terms of the non-human, of what he calls Things (*Dinge*), a way of thought which, as he himself pointed out, is more characteristic of the child than of the adult. To the former, tables, dolls, houses, trees, dogs, etc., have a life which is just as real as their own or that of their parents. Indeed, as a rule children think of life in terms of things and animals rather than in terms of people: a conscious interest in people does not commonly begin until adolescence.[2]

In Auden's view, to see "the human in terms of the non-human" does not necessarily deprive it of its humanity but throws a fresh light on it that keeps us from pursuing blindly our ordinary, uncriticized life of sensation. Abstraction of this kind—not the usual bland abstraction of intellectual discourse, but the introduction of surprising allegorical perspectives (people as country-sides, internal conflicts as military strategies)—is not cold and remote but suffused with feeling. For the child the things, the *Dinge* of which Rilke speaks, are "sacred," filled with mana and meaning, and not only the things but their names, so that a mispronunciation (like the *pirrits* of Auden's aunt) seems blasphemous. On the other hand, it was not blasphemous for the aunt; since she did not share his idea of the sacred, she could not blaspheme against it: "One cannot be taught to recognize a sacred being, one has to be converted." (*DH*, 56) This problem is precisely the poet's—to make what is sacred to him sacred to the reader, or, by praising his own sacred objects, to remind the reader of his.

The first course presents obvious difficulties: if any particular being or event is sacred to A and not to B, how can they share the verbal rite of poetry, which, says Auden, "pays homage by naming?" (*DH*, 57) Is naming enough? The moon or darkness or death may, as he says, be sacred to us all; but their *names* are not necessarily so. It would appear that what the poet must therefore do—if he wants to pay homage, say, to the moon—is not to pronounce the word but to find images, phrases, and rhythms that will make us somehow feel the sacredness of his own encounter with the moon.

Since the moon, he says, is sacred to us all, his presentation of his encounter with it justifies itself. But, if his encounter is with some more special object whose sacredness the rest of us do not feel (lead mines, for example), then what must come through for us (or the poem fails) is some quality or pattern of feeling common to sacred encounters generally (or to certain kinds of them), so that we recognize in the poet's awe for lead mines the same sense of significance that for us is located, say, in attics.

Thus, even though Auden's *Dinge* are different from ours, his *naming* of them is a rite of homage that we can share, for naming —apostrophe, invocation, celebration—is a universal human impulse. And how he loves to name! Anyone acquainted with his verse knows his passion for lists: "Newman, Ciddy, Plato, Fronny, Pascal, Bowdler, Baudelaire,/Doctor Frommer, Mrs. Allom, Freud, the Baron, and Flaubert . . ." (*1930*, XXII); "The child, the waterfall, the fire, the stone . . ." (*CP*, 35); "The nights, the railway-arches, the bad sky . . ." (*CP*, 121); and even for repetitive syntactical devices: appositives, variations, and parallel sentence structure. One example should suffice—one in which almost every new phrase picks up and varies an earlier phrase, with the effect almost of a ritual dance, whose slow progress forward even mimics the speaker's reluctance to give up the society dying around him:

> You whom I gladly walk with, touch,
> Or wait for as one certain of good,
> We know it, we know that love
> Needs more than the admiring excitement of union,
> More than the abrupt self-confident farewell,
> The heel on the finishing blade of grass,
> The self-confidence of the falling root,
> Needs death, death of the grain, our death,
> Death of the old gang. . . . (*CP*, 67)

Auden seems to take, even for a poet, an extraordinary delight in such significant repetition (witness his gluttonous appetite for rhyme-schemes and verse forms). To say something's name and then to say it again satisfies his invocational passion. Indeed, his poems, religious or not, are full of invocations, explicit and implied, invocations to various figures—God, famous writers, abstract ideas, the superego, the life instincts, any felt source of power. Before he believes in a God to call on, he turns naturally to prayers, litanies, choruses, hymns. Isherwood writes in 1937: "When we collaborate, I have to keep a sharp eye on him—or down flop the characters on their knees. . . . If Auden had his way, he would turn every play into a cross between grand opera and high mass."[3]

If to call on a man's name is to secure his power for one's own side, how much more effective to possess his style or his stanza! Thus, another form of invocation is the imitation or parody, for even Auden's parody is usually affectionate. Its extent, too, is almost bizarre. Surely no English poet—Eliot nor Pope nor Jonson—echoes so many sources. And Auden not only acknowledges this feature of his own work but recommends to young poets that they choose masters, one at a time, and learn to do recognizable imitations of each, which involves "attending to every detail of his diction, rhythms and habits of sensibility." (*DH*, 38)

The English language itself in all its forms sometimes seems the chief theme of his praise. As he puts it much later: "Whatever else it may or may not be, I want every poem I write to be a hymn in praise of the English language: hence my fascination with certain speech-rhythms which can only occur in an uninflected language rich in monosyllables, my fondness for peculiar words with no equivalents in other tongues, and my deliberate avoidance of that kind of visual imagery which has no basis in verbal experience and can therefore be translated without loss."[4] Hence, too, his imitations of the diction of jukebox love songs, political speeches, the Book of Common Prayer, officialese, sermons, letters, diaries, wills, hymns, petitions, reveries, and curses. It seems sometimes as if Auden had set himself the task of imitating any kind of English speech, any use of English words.

As for his verse forms, they are far too numerous to list because almost every poem Auden writes is original in form. Even when he repeats a form, as in his sonnets or his syllabic verse, something is altered from poem to poem—the rhyme scheme or the pattern of stresses or syllables. Every poem, therefore, is a new ceremony, its form springing out of the new material, or even shaping that material—Logos and Eros again fusing (if successful, if watched over by Agape) to celebrate something, to say its name.

III *Realm and Realm*

To say the name of something, to pay homage to it, is what Auden's poetry tries to do. The thing itself can never exist on the page, or in the voice; but if the words are right, they can become to others, too, a *name* for the thing, or for things of its kind. Invocation is a sacred process, by which Auden's feeling for *his* things may parallel our feeling for ours, his celebration be shared by us. These sacred forms of appeal, basic in his work, also dramatize his sense of reality as issuing out of significant confrontations between different levels of experience—inner and outer, psychological and social, the world of ordinary surfaces and the inner, anxious, stricken soul, Myself and the Other.

Almost all his poetry pits one such realm against another, not to show the superiority of one but to emphasize the constant unexpectedness of life, the way one world has of opening up to reveal another: it is only through such confrontations that we see things in a new light, and new light is all the light there is. Wherever life is most ordinary, there the miracle is most likely to happen, the conditional world to be surprised by the Unconditional. Beneath the surfaces of life lies the Freudian id, or the Marxist pattern of history, or the Incarnation; the ordinary and the miraculous, time and eternity, Eros and Agape, are different sides of the flashing, surprising world, where the chief events are these changes in perspective. In such circumstances naming and invoking are means of opening doors to this more real realm where the meanings are at play.

His poetry is always most successful, therefore, when the changes of perspective are most skillfully managed. In all his best work the structure of dislocation is implicit in the poem's form, or in the ironic disproportion of form to situation. In his later poems, as we shall see, he builds these ironic structures with special care. The abstract poems, on the other hand, often fail to reach us, I think, because their structures lack perspectival variety. The mutual illumination of realm and realm, abstract and concrete, is intermittent. The straightforward discussion dips down too little into "the ponds of apperception"; and the subtle observations on human life are not reinforced by our sense of some significant relation between the observer and his occasions —that is, by tone.

Certainly there are moments when Auden's abstract poems do exhibit that sudden accession of "the world's body," when the actual rises out of the surrounding plateau of abstraction, as in the dramatic finale of "In Time of War": ". . . night's tiny noises/Will echo vivid in the owl's developed ear . . ." (*CP*, 346); or, from "The Quest" (1940): "The nights came padding after him like wild/Beasts that meant harm, and all the doors cried Thief. . . ." (*CP*, 254) But too often the poems remain in the one realm; references to the actual world do not quite carry us to it; the objects do not get through to us as objects, but only as words for objects: "The hour-glass whispers to the lion's paw,/The clock-towers tell the gardens day and night,/How many errors Time has patience for,/How wrong they are in being always right." (*CP*, 118)

Despite the sly humor, we are not at all moved; we feel no encounter with anything important; we do not really get into the world of lions and gardens, whereas when Destiny steals behind the chest of drawers in Rilke's poem, the effect is startling. For in Rilke the discussion of the inner life in abstract terms is balanced by the extraordinarily urgent tone, often agonized, always supremely warm, quivering with a humanity we feel he shares with us. Auden's tone, on the other hand, in the very poems that owe most to Rilke, is detached, unruffled, observant. And even his few successful invasions of the actual are not sustained, as Rilke's are, through a whole Rilkean poem.

Thus, statement is not enough; abstraction is not enough. For Auden's poetry has as its central action the process of exchange (disguise, hostility, conversion) between realms of existence, usually between the actual and some more significant and fundamental but abstract realm. In his successful poems this exchange is dramatized (named) variously, the abstract realm being conveyed through allegorical imagery or by intellectual formulation, the actual through concrete imagery and personal tone. But the poems fail when, however clever the abstract formulation, the realm of the actual is presented too weakly to serve as a fitting antagonist to the abstract, when the shifts in perspective show us nothing important.

111

John G. Blair, in his fine book on Auden, maintains that virtually all of Auden's principal poetic techniques are allegorical, that they deliberately prevent us from paying excessive attention to particular objects, scenes, persons, even feelings, in order to direct our attention always to the general case. Hence the lists, the skipping imagery, the suppression of articles, the allegorized landscape, and similar devices that encourage us to look for the general principle that links a series of actualities.[5] It may be added that, instead of allowing us to identify smugly with some speaker who is feeling deeply but vaguely and irresponsibly, Auden permits identification only with speakers who are quietly and unpretentiously becoming aware of truths. Learning, beginning to see something—this is almost the only pattern of feeling which Auden judges his poetry has a right to ask the reader to share—except, of course, the joy that follows such insight, the pleasure of seeing the world in a new perspective. Since Auden in his later work is at pains not to overstate any emotion in which he wants his reader to participate, this joy and pleasure are never accompanied by the grandiose orchestration with which almost all Romantic poets, even Eliot and Yeats, often overwhelm the reader.

Throughout the late 1930's and early 1940's Auden is still working out just how poetry can be written that may move and urge and yet not drown. Much of it, at first, in its caution not to drown, seems to move too little and to urge too much. The search for generality leads to a forbidding abstraction; even where we can accept a language almost entirely conceptual, we still wish for some hint of a human person in the tone. But it should be clear by now, as we watch Auden explore the possibilities open to him in the years following the formulation of his mature ethics and aesthetic, that, far from being the uncommitted, frivolous, trivial poet that hostile critics have found him because they misunderstand his political and religious ideas and his assertions about the "frivolity" of art, Auden in his later career has been unfailingly constant and serious in his pursuit of an honest poetics and of poems that reach the reader without victimizing him.[6]

CHAPTER 13

A Place to Stand

A UDEN'S PRINCIPAL WORK between 1940 and 1947 consists of four long poems: "New Year Letter," *For the Time Being, The Sea and the Mirror,* and *The Age of Anxiety.* Although critics differ in their preferences, most agree that at least one of these poems is brilliant and at least one is painfully bad; opinions about "New Year Letter" and *The Age of Anxiety* have been particularly mixed. All four poems continue the progression I have noted in *Another Time* from cosmic, detached abstraction toward the warmth of closer engagement in ordinary life. The issues are still very large, but the tone is often more personal: we find people before us who breathe their hopes and regrets. The general outlook, too, is much brighter than in the despairing works of the later 1930's. And the verse achieves unprecedented elegance; while the tones of the speakers become more informal, even colloquial, their verse settings grow more operatic. At their worst, these poems are distinguished by a glossy, brittle quality; at their best, by a radiant splendor. Auden's treatment of the *ordinary* life of man is either grandly offhand or deftly grave.

Auden is able to take such stances, accurately reflecting the ambiguities and contradictions of our complex life, because of the elaborate stylized structures that these poems present. Simple as some of them seem in design, all of them are supported by extensive scaffoldings of philosophical irony. Each work presents a multiplicity of contradictory attitudes; one basic contradiction is that between the ordinary human desire for simplicity, directness and clarity and the intelligent man's awareness of the need for irony and qualification. Human truth is the product of incongruities, of distorted perspectives, of surprising analogies—Caliban as Henry James, St. Joseph as a character out of Saroyan, the Faerie Queene in a Third Avenue bar.

What Auden basically does—here as elsewhere—is to construct

113

a bizarre situation, composed of elements we do not expect to see in each other's company, and then allow the characters (or the speaker) to behave normally, taking for granted what is odd in their situations or in their own styles, and within these limitations carrying on with relative simplicity. In effect, Auden's personages, provided with apparently inappropriate styles by their apparently whimsical creator, accept the necessity of the Kierkegaardian leap of faith. As human life is absurd but can only be affirmed and embraced, so too the provisional life of these characters is accepted by them as inexplicable but given; their verse forms, their dictions, are modes which, like the social and physical conditions of our own life, cannot be evaded but must be used as the medium of each man's salvation.

Throughout these poems, too, it *is* the working out of one's own salvation that is most often central. Auden no longer sees any likelihood that socialism or any secular solution or, indeed, any foreseeable religious transformation will shortly redeem the whole world. Hence his poetry no longer urges the reader to the disciplined love and concerted action that seemed desirable in his more Marxist frame of mind. Secular reform is not now *un*desirable, but Auden's emphasis has returned to where it was in his early poems and to where it had always been straining to return: to the individual anxiety, to the progress of the ordinary human soul toward health or God. Now, however, his presentation of this ordinary soul is strengthened by his having arrived at a mature and consistent view of life and art, a complex and yet flexible point of view from which he may survey, describe, and interpret the patterns of everyday behavior—patterns of outer activity and of inner *malaise*.

Where Auden's early poetry badgered the reader to choose between normal illness and healthy rebellion, or later between conventional evil and Socialist community, and still later simply faced him with the ghastly spectre of a dead world, the poetry of the 1940's and after urges upon the reader the possibility of becoming himself, the person he is capable of being. There is little or nothing of the schoolmaster's tone in these later works; instead of the direct plea or the pointed presentation that accuses the reader and requires him to renounce and choose (as in much of the work down to 1934 or so), and instead even of the logical analysis that implicitly tells the reader what side to take (as in the 1937-38 period), the later poems tactfully limit themselves to exposure of certain speakers' positions. When the accusing finger makes its appearance now, it is only as part of an ironic pose. As the character or speaker on view explains his position or arrives at a new one, we are invited to be present at his artistic apotheosis and to let its brilliance, its meaning, illuminate our lives. But all this is carried on now with elaborate discretion, with a classical concern for our delicate sensibilities, as if the poet were at pains not to let it be seen too baldly that the lives whose mistakes and weakness he permits to appear before us are, in fact, emblems of our own.

This new tact is largely due to Auden's having found new principles of construction for his longer works. The Brechtian challenge to the audience has given way to the Kierkegaardian exposure of the truth: for any man whom poetry is likely to reach, truth is sufficient challenge. In any case, the method is appropriate to the poetry of a man who believes in the voluntary penitential way. Grace is something conferred from outside, yet one must will to be ready to receive it. Hence the poetry is not to be read without a certain effort; its riddles are sometimes difficult; its language, its syntax, its references, even its rhythms, may have to be worked at a bit. When all is done, illumination may or may not reward the effort. Poetry can only, at most, present "An abstract model of events/Derived from dead experience,/And each life must itself decide/To what and how it be applied." (*DM*,* 20) Interpretations may differ; still, the symbols are tied, not loosely suggestive; the structures are systematic; the "abstract model" yields its meanings to methodical study.

The Kierkegaardian attitude is supported, furthermore, by the formal structures Auden uses in these four poems—structures which owe much, as Edward Callan has shown,[1] to Kierkegaardian categories of thought, especially to the triad of attitudes already discussed: the Aesthetic, Ethical, and Religious. In conjunction with other organizing frameworks, this dynamic scheme —in which the first two categories, insufficient but necessary ingredients of the modern whole man, are reconciled and made fruitful only upon the acceptance of the third—provides a solid basis not merely for these four poems but for most of Auden's later verse.

In particular, this scheme gives to this work a unity lacking

The Double Man (New York, 1941).

in the earlier, for the earlier establishes no consistent ground of value; it keeps observing the patterns of twentieth-century human reality, but from constantly shifting positions that are strongest when they condemn and assail but that often become blurred and false in feeling when they propose. Auden, running in his early years from mentor to mentor, from country to country, from style to style, from hat to hat, becomes emblematic himself of a certain cultural displacement: a visitor everywhere, nowhere quite at home, Auden the uprooted, the Wanderer, the refugee. Christianity gives him a place to stand. Once it is his, the verse becomes more sure even as it becomes less cocksure.

Thus, where the old, attacking, exposing poetry was constantly faced with the unspoken question, "All right, if that is evil, what is good?" and could devise only relatively unconvincing or negative replies ("Love!" or "Don't be Romantic, don't be dishonest" —good advice as far as it went), now, far from hedging at these crucial junctures, Auden's poetry, as it moves to its conclusions, begins to do so with a kind of triumphant joy. As the end approaches and the art gets ready to release us again into life, we are invited to share a double pleasure—pleasure in the fineness of the work itself, so elegantly contrived and richly developed, and pleasure, too, in the splendor of life, with all its marvelous patterns, and especially with its art and its intelligence crowned, improbably but absolutely, by its religious coherence.

We need not even, it seems to me, accept Auden's religious views in order to share the pleasure he takes in life, for his view does not minimize evil: he is aware of it, he writes about it, he finds it in himself as in others. But as submission to the Unconscious was urged by his early verse, and submission to History by his verse of the 1930's, what he advises now is submission to our own time and place and possibilities—to the limitations inherent in our being human. Given such submission to the Necessity of life's conditions, we are then free to observe, to use our senses, to play with art, to exercise our intellect, even to perform our civic duty. We are free to do what, in fact, we must do: to love our neighbor. Auden's old convictions are by no means all discarded; the basic ones remain, only to be given new meaning by a new framework. The Christian setting amplifies echoes of Homer Lane: "If a man does not love mankind and the universe, he is not true to his nature. Man does not choose to love; he *must* love."[2]

116

CHAPTER 14

Person and Quest

I *"New Year Letter"*

THE FIRST of these four long poems, "New Year Letter" (1941), seems, after *Another Time*, remarkably hopeful. The simple diction, the melodic ease, and the quietly cheerful outlook of the last poems in *Another Time* are developed and deepened here. Affirmative, relaxed, urbane, loyal always to its colloquial base of the chatty, ranging, witty letter, this survey of contemporary feeling and thought is still intensely serious, sometimes solemn. The verse itself (octosyllabic couplets) is a modern marvel: the phrasing and rhyming are almost always easy and natural; the danger of monotony is reduced not only by Auden's epigrammatic ingenuity but by the long and complex sentences that, together with the occasional difficulty of ideas or allusions, guard against the possible feeling that art, history, and life are being oversimplified. Frequent changes of pace, style, or mood quicken the poem again and again, and so does the constant shift from personal to public concerns. If the values of such verse—its dazzling clarities of sound and sense—are nowadays subordinated to our taste for irregular rhythms and images that explode from inside, it still seems likely that "New Year Letter" will one day seem a classic of our time.

According to Edward Callan's analysis,[1] the three sections of the poem correspond to Kierkegaard's Aesthetic, Ethical, and Religious categories; as Auden reviews the metaphysical limitations of Art and Reason in the face of contemporary troubles, and shows at last how nothing can save us but knowledge of ourselves, humility, confession of our sins, and acceptance of what God gives, the poem marks out the stages of conversion. Part III, in particular, as it ponders Auden's own relation to English landscape and the history of man since the Renaissance, seems

117

to turn finally both to a rational recognition of the necessity of dispensing with pride and to that impulse to invoke which is never far from Auden and which here embodies the imperative of the leap of faith: *O da quod jubes, Domine.*

The poem is dated January 1, 1940, but was not published until March, 1941; in that time Auden was converted, so that the poem's movement from its relatively jaunty and secular tone at the beginning to Christian injunctions and Christian invocation at the end seems entirely appropriate. What gives particular life to the poem is the personal tone that keeps warming the abstractions and the learned tour of history and literature. We feel always that the intellectuality is swept with feeling, that the search for meaning, for ground, is a suffering, human search, and that even the speaker's leap of faith at the end is validated by the seriousness and honesty, even by the air of exhaustiveness (he has really looked everywhere), which, beneath the urbanity, have throughout characterized his quest.

It is difficult to illustrate this personal warmth, for it is something we feel as we read through long passages which, however abstract they become, almost always return to the personal note. The abstract complexities are not just fascinating puzzles but truths that distress or encourage a human being. We see him turning in various directions as he seeks guidance in the good life, or we see the results of his having so turned. Art, he shows us first, can do much, can offer us a model of the way things are; but "Art is not life and cannot be/A midwife to society." (*CP*, 267) The "great masters" of the past "have shown mankind/An order it has yet to find" (*CP*, 268), but they cannot reorganize our lives for us; at best, the poet now can show us our own disorder.

Reason, too, as we see in the second section, has severe limitations; still, it has its uses. The instinctive life certainly offers us much, but we cannot trust it entirely. We should be aware that life as we actually experience it emotionally is different from the measuring order of time, that "all our intuitions mock/The formal logic of the clock./All real perception, it would seem,/Has shifting contours like a dream. . . ." (*CP*, 278) But we are mistaken if we therefore "throw away intelligence" and give ourselves over to instinct. Indeed, this is the greater danger. Modern man suffers from the double lie of Plato and Rousseau (*cf.* "September

1, 1939")—the "lie of intellect" that resigns authority and responsibility to the philosopher-kings, and the "falsehood of the
flesh" by virtue of which we think we are all equal because we
have equal access to the world of feeling.

Both lies, in Auden's view, encourage us to do as we please, to
embrace any or all experience, and to forfeit the standards by
which we might evaluate and choose. The result is Wagner and
his Tristan, an operatic, unredeeming nightmare from which
nothing can release us but submission to the facts of life, acceptance of human limitations. In human experience, art can give
us a foretaste of the perfection of Heaven, but it is Hell to expect
life to be like that. Ordinary life is, rather, Purgatory, a constant
struggle in which we are tested, through which we may be
really redeemed.

Through all these truths and "half-truths we can synthesise"
(*CP*, 289) the human speaker seeks to "Ascend the penitential
way" (*CP*, 294), to reconcile all those doublenesses and multiplicities in himself which, like intelligence and feeling, exert
rival claims upon him. The original American edition of the poem
was, in fact, called *The Double Man,* and the doubleness refers
not only to the Aesthetic and Ethical realms and to the opposition
of thought and feeling, but to other polarities inherent in being
human. As this discussion has already indicated, the poem
moves continually between the abstract and the personal; it jogs
back and forth as well between personal and public life. We all
live, Auden tells us, in two worlds:

> There are two atlases: the one
> The public space where acts are done,
> In theory common to us all,
> Where we are needed and feel small
>
> . . . .
>
> The other is the inner space
> Of private ownership, the place
> That each of us is forced to own,
> Like his own life from which it's grown . . . (*CP*, 296)

The poem tries to balance this doubleness, too, as it discusses
matters important to Auden personally—as a poet, a friend, an
Englishman come to America—and affairs in the public world:
Europe as it is now and as it has been since the Renaissance. In

treating this various material, Auden adopts the tone of the civilized man of letters, an Englishman writing in America to a German woman about culture, history, and art. He alludes casually to such literary works and authors and to such ideas and historical events as educated people presumably are familiar with; and he drops words and phrases in French, German, Latin, Italian, and Greek. His perspective—that of the European tradition—inevitably imposes order on the diverse matters that he takes up. The *"civitas* of sound" that results from playing Buxtehude, the *polis* that is made up of friends (*CP*, 266, 295)— these are the images that European civilization can provide of the good life—and the octosyllabic couplets are a fitting measure to order his perceptions and insights.

The final acceptance of a Western history given to error but ultimately overseen by a Christian God is one of the central doublenesses of this poem, in which Auden seems to have been thinking of himself as sharing that "belief-in-disbelief" that Charles Williams attributes to Montaigne.[2] Indeed, Montaigne provides the volume's epigraph: "We are, I know not how, double in ourselves, so that what we believe we disbelieve, and cannot rid ourselves of what we condemn." By the end of the poem it has become clear to the speaker that the "situation of our time" (*CP*, 271) can be resolved only in belief, belief that "every day in sleep and labour/Our life and death are with our neighbour,/And love illuminates again/The city and the lion's den,/The world's great rage, the travel of young men." (*CP*, 316)

For the poem, always controlled by the personal tone, has been fundamentally an account, logical rather than chronological, of the speaker's travels, especially of his intellectual travels through the past and present, the Europe and America of feeling and thought. With all the elegant motions of a chivalric romance, "New Year Letter" reports his quest—its adventures and its success.

II *Addenda*

The poem is most effective by itself, but it appeared in *The Double Man* (British edition: *New Year Letter*), in company with certain other writing that presumably was meant to locate or explain or reinforce it:

1) A Prologue ("Spring 1940" in *CP*) and an Epilogue ("Autumn 1940" in *CP*), both in rather prosy syllabic verse. The Prologue can only lament the present trouble, but the Epilogue arrives at the possibility of prayer.

2) Notes—and not just a few explanatory observations, but a jumble of quotations, citations, comments, poetic jottings, sonnets—altogether a messy assortment of random effluvia on most of the subjects dealt with so neatly in the "Letter." Here again, perhaps, is a doubleness, the wild disorder lurking behind the stately scene. But the disorder quite overwhelms the stage; the "Letter's" sixty-two pages fall away before eighty-four pages of Notes. Where in *Letters from Iceland* mess and order were all thrown together, here they are side by side; in the later long works the disorder will be invisible, a realm of existence to be conveyed not by disorder itself but elegantly: we know what Caliban is even while he talks like Henry James.

3) "The Quest," a sequence of twenty sonnets, first published in November, 1940, which means that Auden probably began it later than "New Year Letter" and finished it earlier. Very different in tone, feeling, and approach, this group of poems touches more explicitly on the same quest-motif that is fundamental to "New Year Letter," and it is closely concerned with the same ethical problems: how to live a good life, a life successful in the deepest sense, how to avoid the wrong kinds of commitment, what one can learn from those who had great gifts and yet failed, what part luck plays in one's success, and so on. As is typical in Auden, the heroic quest becomes a metaphor for ordinary life and its crucial but inconspicuous choices; it is one of his frequent themes that the heroic event, or the experience of significant suffering, occurs "nowhere particularly unusual" (*CP*, 82), "While someone else is eating or opening a window or just walking dully along. . . . (*CP*, 3)

So, as the couplets of "New Year Letter" swing from the personal to the public atlas in an attempt to survey Auden's own important relationships (to art, to England and America, to European civilization, to intellect, and to friends), the Rilkean sonnets of "The Quest," both less personal and less public, generalize the various patterns of relationship that may exist among such elements of a man's life as temperament, talent, training, and desires on the one hand, and, on the other, the immediate conditions. It becomes clear that every man's quest is different, and its chances of success depend on the adaptation of his gifts to the particular situations that confront him (or that he *is* from time to time).

We are told differently in our childhoods, of course; we are given lists of virtues that everyone is to acquire:

> In villages from which their childhoods came
> Seeking Necessity, they had been taught
> Necessity by nature is the same,
> No matter how or by whom it be sought.

The city of adulthood, on the contrary "welcomed each as if he came alone,/The nature of Necessity like grief/Exactly corresponding to his own." (*CP*, 253) If there is in this series, as in "In Time of War," a certain disjunctiveness—so that no sonnet seems quite to begin where the last has left off, and all are in different forms—it is because in life we all pursue our own journeys simultaneously, in sight of one another yet alone. The abstract arrangement corresponds, therefore, to the obscurity and isolation of the individual quest.

Still, it *is* abstract; the tone stays even and without urgency; the dispassionate diagnostician observes the diagrammatic configurations of the inner, anxious world and of its encounters with outer conditions—observes and epigrammatically reports, and the result, though often witty, is also chilling. The classical externality of "New Year Letter" is balanced by the warmth of feeling throughout, by our sense of the man at the center of the poem who moves from his intellectual formulations to remarks about his own life, fears, worries, friends. Like so many other poems of this era in Auden's career, "The Quest" proceeds from a nameless expositor who seems not to share the life he describes.

"The Quest" is the last extended work to use this disembodied speaker, and "New Year Letter" clearly shows us why. From now on Auden characteristically locates his abstractions within a feeling frame so that they are felt as occasions of feeling, as affective elements in a structure of feelings. Not the poet himself but his securely dramatized speaker experiences these abstractions, and we watch what happens. This dramatic structure occurs in earlier poems, of course, but in no consistent way; in the ballads and in certain poems with dramatized personae, the dynamic relationship between the speaker and his situation, which he often misreads, fascinates us. Auden's best poems—and the best effects in other poems—tend to be of this kind. But only around the time of "New Year Letter" does he seem consciously to center his poetry in the dramatized reception of new understanding. Not simply truth, but *a man seeing a truth,* is henceforth the central situation in his work.

Does this development involve a radical shift from Auden's old anti-Romantic position? Not necessarily: the poet still need not present his own private life, and even the details that he does present may be chosen for their effectiveness in exhibiting some *general* truth. But it is nonetheless true that the example of man most familiar to the poet is himself; and, as we shall see— not in the long works of the 1940's but increasingly in the more ambitious shorter poems—Auden opens his life and his mind more and more to public view. For the moment, in other long poems, he sees what can be done with less personal forms, but even in these highly stylized works the movement toward per- sonal illumination (Kierkegaardian and Jamesian) remains the characteristic mode.

CHAPTER 15

Three Pageants

I F "NEW YEAR LETTER" dramatizes its speaker and his quest, the three other long poems of the 1940's are even more fully and more formally dramatic. Variously mannered, suggesting analogies with other arts, especially with opera, they are, in Blair's term, "semi-dramas—longer works which assume stage conventions but are intended primarily for reading."[1] Each semi-drama is constructed as a series of tableaux which we feel as both static and dynamic: the juxtaposition of the panels pleases us, but we sense as we proceed that the issues are deepening, and that between the beginning and the end a significant development has taken place. Just how this progress occurs varies with the form: *For the Time Being* is, Auden tells us, a "Christmas Oratorio," *The Sea and the Mirror* a "Commentary on Shakespeare's *The Tempest*," and *The Age of Anxiety* a "Baroque Eclogue." Each therefore calls for a different basic diction and for different principles of arrangement.[2]

I *Oratorio*

For the Time Being is a lively pageant of choruses, recitatives, arias, and prose speeches; it is divided into tableaux like the old mystery cycles and possesses, as Edward Callan has shown,[3] an elaborate philosophical structure. The characters, in medieval fashion, present themselves directly to the audience and explain or dramatize their attitudes and situations. The verse often has a Romanesque innocence: "*Let us run to learn/How to love and run;/Let us run to Love.*" (*CP*, 440)

Since *this* semi-drama may be performed as well as read, the arias and choruses are usually set in rather plain English. Auden thus has the problem—the same that he had faced in the mid-1930's when he had tried to give flat speech extra resonance (see

Chapter 6)—of making the truly simple reverberate with meaning and yet not sound insipid. One course open to him is to change pace frequently in order to keep the familiar story of Christ's nativity brisk and animated; he therefore writes the parts in a variety of verse forms. Since he wishes to show the Nativity from all angles, he is free to throw in some lively satiric pieces on the secular world at the time of Christ; these are, of course, updated so that their objects have recognizable contemporary counterparts. The Incarnation, after all, has both inner and social contexts. Deliberate anachronisms suggest the presentness of these events, for the significance of the Incarnation is less that it happened once than that it is always happening.

The central subject of the piece is the meeting of the ordinary and the miraculous. Mary, Joseph, the Shepherds, even the Wise Men, are all ordinary human beings; Herod himself is an ordinary liberal reformer; and the appearance of the extraordinary among them is the fact to which they must adjust their ordinary perceptions, fears, and desires. For Auden, the Incarnation is at the very center of his metaphysical speculation; for its reconciliation of divinity and humanity is analogous to the reconciliation of the abstract and the concrete, Logos and Eros, event and meaning. It might be thought, then, that of all subjects the Incarnation should be the most perfectly suited to his talents and intellectual concerns.

Alas, not so. Apart from his plays, *For the Time Being* seems to me the least successful of his longer works. For one thing, its echoes of Eliot and Yeats are much too bland, obvious, and lacking in irony. Auden's assimilation of the method of *The Waste Land* in his early verse and of that of *Four Quartets* in his later is much more subtle and original than his adaptation in *For the Time Being* of the later poems and the early plays.

Yet even after the echoes die away, as they mainly do after the first two or three tableaux, the problem of simplicity remains; the textures are too smooth and continuous; and, although the characters must be stylized, they still seem too thin, too little human. In this story of the Incarnation, the meeting in Christ of God and Man, the godly element is well represented by a multitude of abstractions; the human is hardly there at all. A heavy philosophical structure rests on a scanty foundation of the convincingly actual. The language of the simple people too often lacks bite and force. Here, for example, is the end of the dialogue between Joseph and Gabriel. Joseph asks:

> How then am I to know,
> Father, that you are just?
> Give me one reason.
>
> ### Gabriel
> No.
>
> ### Joseph
> All I ask is one
> Important and elegant proof
> That what my Love had done
> Was really at your will
> And that your will is Love.
>
> ### Gabriel
> No, you must believe;
> Be silent, and sit still. (*CP*, 424)

Too much of the verse is equally inactive, without notable verbal interest; it is not memorable speech. What is true of the words is true of the people; they are generalized and dull: Mary, sweet and gentle; Joseph, confused and obedient; Herod, whose decision to massacre the innocents is represented as the logical conclusion to a career of liberal reform; the Wise Men, Gilbert-and-Sullivanesque versions of the scientist, metaphysician, and political economist; and the Shepherds, who stand for the proletariat. Nothing individual marks off one character from another; they all represent some abstract position.

Spears, who finds the oratorio in general "a unique and remarkable success both formally and as a whole" and is pleased with "the enormous scope and variety of the piece" (217), thinks the section on the shepherds "would be enough to confute those who say Auden lacks understanding of or sympathy with the common man; it is shrewd, amusing, and without condescension." (212) But the moment the shepherds appear, it is evident from what they say that they are a special class, poorer than the rest of us, with duller (though crucially necessary) jobs, and with certain shrewd insights; Auden's observation is not shrewd really, but is an observation of the shepherds' shrewdness. The significant thing about them, says one of the shepherds, "is that each of us is waiting." And another goes on: "That is why we are able to bear/Ready-made clothes, second-hand art and opinions/ And being washed and ordered about. . . ." (*CP*, 437) Not condescending?

Later, another shepherd says: "The solitude familiar to the poor/Is feeling that the family next door,/The way it talks, eats, dresses, loves, and hates,/Is indistinguishable from one's own." (*CP*, 443) Far from being shrewd or uncondescending, this view of the poor is the one an outsider has—not a view that the poor have of themselves. It is only from outside that the poor—or the rich, or Chinese, or poets—look all alike; for familiarity breeds distinction as well as contempt. Besides, the feeling that the family next door is like one's own does not foster solitude but community, except in the person who, resenting his family's ordinariness, is convinced of his own individual uniqueness. But this conviction is not felt generally by the poor; it is most common among individuals who are not poor.[4]

The fault here is one that Auden has never overcome. His characters must all be stylized, all but one. For he can present feelingly, from inside, only the hesitant, sophisticated, anxious modern man taking stock of his situation and wondering where to go next. The best approach he can make to simplicity is to present a complex mind in a simple state, or to show the simple personage from the outside in a characteristic revealing gesture or pose. Hence the generic categories in which his poetry abounds: the lovers, the soldiers, the women, the shepherds, all of whom he categorizes with a sweeping assurance that their background position often justifies. But when the simple types move into the foreground, as they often do in the plays and in *For the Time Being*, they do not convince, because Auden, in drawing them nearer to us, has not seen more deeply into them. His only successful alternative is to satirize them by exaggerating still more the gestures and poses we can see from a distance, and in *For the Time Being* all the best pieces are satiric. But the truly simple seems beyond Auden's ability to dramatize. Aware as we are, even from indications within this oratorio, of the remarkable sophistication of Auden's mind, his attempt to portray the simplicity of these "common ungifted/Natures" (*CP*, 428), though it recalls the graceful naïveté of the medieval Nativity play, must seem, in comparison, at best disingenuous.

Aside from the unconvincing primitivism of *For the Time Be-*

ing, its force rests too heavily on the doctrines that not only lie behind the whole drama but intrude again and again in devout phrases, often liturgical—phrases that, we suspect, Auden was rediscovering at this time and whose newfound freshness to his own ears he hoped to convey to ours. But, despite the success of a few pieces and the childlike charm of much of the work, *For the Time Being* has little of that human force that distinguishes the best religious poetry: the people are not really people, the sin not really sin; and the exchange between heaven and earth is, therefore, a kind of stylish puppet show. To take the work as simply that is probably enough; to claim for it as much as Spears does is to invite dissent from all those for whom neither the holy phrases nor the Christian fable is sacred in any sense.

II *Triptych*

If *For the Time Being* offers little to those who reject its doctrines, *The Sea and the Mirror* offers much. In it Auden again allows his characters to face us directly and explain their attitudes. One by one the principals of Shakespeare's *The Tempest* step forward to speak, each in a different form, of their common experience and their private hopes, of their wishes and their disappointments, and of the meanings that they now see in what is behind and before them. If there is one thing they all share, it is a kind of radiance; they have all been touched by magic; in their words there is a shining; in their tones, moderated differently in each and missing only in Antonio, there is a joy. They step to the edge of the stage as if in a trance of exaltation, of heightened awareness of their lives and their lives' meanings. Their speeches—each governed by its formal mode (terza rima, sonnet, ballade, syllabic verse, sestina, villanelle, and others)— are frequently abstract and elliptical, but appropriately so, for these self-declarations seem visionary glimpses into the meaning of what the characters are and have become. And if they are not entirely Shakespeare's people any more, especially in their developed religious consciousness, the polish of the verse and the richness of their reconciliations make them not unworthy transformations of the Shakespearean into the Audenesque.

The main theme of the work is the relation of Art to Life, and its structure (again it is Edward Callan who has pointed out the analogies) owes something to both painting and Kierke-gaard. Callan writes:

> The structure of this poem is comparable to a triptych: the first panel represents the artist; the second, the work of art; and the third, the audience. In Part I, Prospero, the "per-sonified type of the creative," becomes aware of death as a reality he cannot conjure with. His farewell to Ariel is de-veloped in three stages analogous to Kierkegaard's triad. Part II is an elaborate pageant corresponding to Prospero's masque in *The Tempest*. The group of characters from Ferdinand to Miranda who are "linked as children in a circle dancing" represent the ideal order possible in art; and the arrangement also suggests a "Utopian" social order as Alonso holds the center and the courtly and rustic characters are proportioned on either side of him between the lovers. The attitude of Antonio who stands withdrawn from the group represents the tension between his Ethical world of "will" and their Aesthetic world of "wish"—a tension present in all Christian art. Part III, "Caliban to the Audience," is an art-ful symposium in which Caliban echoes the Ethical and Aesthetic attitudes of the audience to the relationship of art and reality.[5]

Caliban's speech does even more. Prospero's, in chatty elegiacs, has raised some of the issues: the life to which he is now return-ing is different from the art he gives up; ethical existence poses problems different from those of the aesthetic order. But Caliban's harangue probes the distinction still more profoundly. In an astonishing reversal of our expectations, the gross Caliban as-sumes several masks in turn but presents the arguments of each in, of all styles, that of the later Henry James. The parody is superb, but it is more than parody: the Jamesian style is just the right one for explaining, with all the necessary qualifications and illustrative digressions, the subtleties and complexities of the points Auden wants to make about Life and Art. None of the prolixity is really superfluous: through all the syntactical extrav-agances, the tone is unfailingly colloquial and animated; and at just the right moments it deepens, in its melodramatic way, to reveal those profundities which it normally seems too capri-cious to reach quite down to. If the characters do not out-Shakespeare Shakespeare, this style out-Jameses James.

Caliban takes up, in his very special fashion, the problems Auden had earlier considered in other works—especially in his reviews and in "New Year Letter." The Sea of life is one thing; the Mirror of art, another. Life is full of disorder, extra paraphernalia, irrelevant perspectives, mess; Art (at least according to the public view, which Caliban begins by voicing) presents only "the perfectly tidiable case of disorder." (*CP*, 378) Its world is one in which everything is patterned; the demands of pattern, in fact, may justify almost any improbability. But in life, pattern is rare and accidental. To introduce real life into art, as Shakespeare has done in creating Caliban, is intolerable, partly because it disturbs art's harmless order, partly because it suggests the corresponding, horrible thought that such aesthetically pleasing ideals as fraternity, romance, and justice might be introduced into life.

Caliban's answer (and Auden's) to this protest is, in effect, that although art and life are different, they are not so entirely cut off from each other as the public and even the usual artist wish to believe. To the would-be poet he explains (on behalf of Shakespeare) that at bottom the image-making faculty (Ariel) is, after all, dependent on the senses, the flesh, and, even deeper than the flesh, the id (Caliban). To the public he explains that their various wishes lead only to despair. The desire to escape from abstraction, from mind, to be completely subjective and to experience only sensations, must end in a totally miscellaneous and undifferentiated perceptiveness, a complete absence of values; it is the "romantic lie in the brain/Of the sensual man in the street" (*AT*,* 100), the error of Don Giovanni, that we have met before.

The other and opposite lie, that of Authority, Tristan's error, is the desire not to be absorbed in the sea of sensation but to be delivered from it to a desert of abstract value; but this world turns out to be equally unsatisfactory, for nothing in it has the kind of identity that can only be given by a concrete context. Clearly, the wish for total absorption or total deliverance in this life is mistaken; and we can find no surer road to despair and grief than to fail to recognize the difference between This Life and "that Wholly Other Life from which we are separated by an

---

Another Time (New York, 1940).

essential emphatic gulf of which our contrived fissures of mirror and proscenium arch . . . are feebly figurative signs. . . ." (*CP*, 402)

Art, whose source is our actual flesh and blood (Yeats's "rag-and-bone shop of the heart"), nevertheless gives us some anticipatory sense of divine perfection: its fidelity to the flesh exposes our actual condition; its formal patterns prefigure divine order and justice. Between the two the human creature wavers, and the artist, "in representing to you your condition of estrangement from the truth, is doomed to fail the more he succeeds, for the more truthfully he paints the condition, the less clearly can he indicate the truth from which it is estranged, the brighter his revelation of the truth in its order, its justice, its joy, the fainter shows his picture of your actual condition in all its drabness and sham. . . ." (*CP*, 399-400)

Whereas in *For the Time Being* the intricate ironic structure of contradictory human impulses, which characterizes all of Auden's best work, had no sufficient material in the simple types of the nativity story, in *The Sea and the Mirror* the simplicities of what are here the minor personages function far more satisfactorily because they are subordinated—and properly, in a work *about* art—to the more complex figures of Prospero, Caliban, and even Alonso. Through most of the first two parts we are invited to understand Auden's general statements about life and art as hard truths or radiant insights achieved by the characters; and, even though Caliban himself, among his several masks, may remain untouched, his language, urbane as it is, often expands the tendency toward melodrama that is inherent in the Jamesian style. Comedy and melodrama steer us unawares into the realm of religious feeling, and the grandness of the subject justifies the excesses of the rhetoric. All the mischief is balanced by classical control, and we are moved by the humanity that speaks through all these masks.

III *Pastoral*

The masks are multiple enough in *The Age of Anxiety*. Stylized characters in varied stances of self-declaration—a basically operatic mode, complicated by occasional duets, quartets, and other elaborate forms—are nowhere more fully in view than in this last of Auden's longer works of the 1940's and so far, except for some later, looser poem-sequences, the last of his extended productions not designed chiefly for the operatic stage. In *The Age of Anxiety* (1947) we are already close to opera: the characters do not speak and then retire (as in *The Sea and the Mirror*), but share a setting and a situation. And, although their personal relationships are somewhat abstract, distant, far from the usual passionate intimacies and entanglements of traditional opera, their musical statements proceed out of a series of psychic experiences which they undergo in concert.

Nowhere, in fact, is Auden's work more severely stylized than in this "baroque eclogue," which at first reading, if we have no key, may appear quite impenetrable. Four persons—Malin, Quant, Rosetta, and Emble—meet on All Souls' Night in a Manhattan bar during World War II. Feeling a certain affinity, they talk, take a booth together, go to Rosetta's apartment for a nightcap, and part at dawn. Their conversation during the night turns on such subjects as "The Seven Ages" and "The Seven Stages"—apparently aspects of human existence—and, at the end of the evening, the sexual attraction felt by Rosetta and Emble comes to nothing as Emble passes out and Rosetta achieves some spiritual realization.

The English of the poem is fantastically elaborate. Auden chooses that one of his favorite verse forms which always sounds archaic—four-stress alliterative verse (here varied by a wealth of other often remarkable forms). But his diction, instead of being that of Old or Middle English, as his earlier practice might lead us to expect, is much more suggestive of Renaissance splendor; for it takes a munificent delight in odd words ("watchet," "meeken," "daedal," "dunlins," "pursive") and in whimsical names of persons ("Major Mott joins Millicent Rusk" [80]) and of places (St Dill-in-the-Deep, St Dust, St Alb,/St Bee-le-Bone, St Botolph-the-less" [10]). This grand but difficult diction, along with the highly symbolic landscape imagery, makes the action seem quite cryptic; and, although we recognize the poem's great elegance, we need guidance in reading it—a map to lead us through the maze, a plan to explain the riddles.

Fortunately, such a plan exists; and again Edward Callan has supplied it.[6] In his study of the allegorical machinery of the poem, we discover that Auden is relying principally on "Jung's concept of the disintegration of the psyche into four differentiated functions. . . ." (155) In *For the Time Being* Auden had presented these briefly under their own names; now he elaborates them into four actual people: Malin is Thought; Rosetta, Feeling; Quant, Intuition; Emble, Sensation. The first two represent evaluative functions of the psyche, the others perceptive functions: "The dramatic action in *The Age of Anxiety* consists of an unfolding in the direction of 'wholeness.' Such change will be most obvious in the evaluative functions, and, therefore, the significant dramatic action will be the raising of feeling to the sphere of consciousness (Rosetta's awakening to the world of reality), and also the freeing of thought from exclusive preoccupation with the rational (a deepening of Malin's vision)." (157)

Thus, "the six parts . . . are six stages in a regenerative journey" (157), of which the two longest and most significant stages are, first, the conscious examination of the epochs of human life ("The Seven Ages") and, second and most important of all, the deeper exploration of the unconscious, both the personal and the collective unconscious ("The Seven Stages"). Through these explorations Rosetta's Feeling and Malin's Thought achieve independently a more mature religious consciousness, and each character arrives at some kind of reconciliation with functions opposite to the one he represents: Malin feels more, Rosetta wakes to thought, Emble in passing out at least ceases to be dominated by sensation, and Quant's *anima* makes him stumble at his own doorstep and become aware of the sensory world: "Why, Miss ME, what's the matter? *Must* you go woolgathering?" (135)

The four characters behave at once realistically and allegorically. The actual events—people meeting in a bar, finding one another's company congenial, and feeling better in the morning because of the levels of themselves that the sudden achievement of temporary communion with others has helped them become aware of—are perfectly ordinary. On the other hand, Auden has deliberately narrowed and deepened his characters' actual lives to fit his allegorical design. If alcohol has made them uncommonly aware of their own feelings and the atmospheres around them, it is Auden, not alcohol, that has given them an uncanny ability to articulate their awarenesses. Hence their explorations of their own pasts and of their own unconsciousnesses (as well as of their collective unconscious) are full of personal touches as the characters remember "Bud and Whitey/And Clifford Monahan and Clem Lifschutz,/Dicky Lamb, Dominic Moreno,/ Svensson, Seidel . . ." (54); and their visions of the unconscious fit their characters. Yet the experience of each is oddly general and impersonal. Although Auden sketches in backgrounds for all of them, they are delivered from specific practical problems; none of them has a parent, a spouse, a child, or even, as far as we know, a significant friend; the situation of all of them is that, ordinary as they are, almost their entire concern is with life in general. Like true Existentialists, like Kierkegaard's Abraham, they are alone with the cosmos, confronted, however casually, by the largest questions. Indeed, although each is a person and at least some of them develop during the action, from another point of view all four make up one composite psyche, that of modern man, whose anxieties spring both from his position as a creature subject to and conscious of time (The Seven Ages, Emble's youth, Quant's age) and from the elemental and largely unconscious guilts, fears, hopes, and joys that give to experiences their peculiar quality.

What Auden seeks to do in *The Age of Anxiety*, then, is to convey the very textures of human experience apart from the ordinary contexts of specific events, objects, social circumstances, practical motives. On the other hand, "pure" emotions or phases of feeling must be translated into a language of objects, persons, and situations. The result is an "abstract" poetry—not with the intellectual abstraction of Auden's discussing poems, but in the tradition of Gertrude Stein or of certain early poems of Ezra Pound. Thus Emble begins his exploration of the unconscious with an almost childish glee in his release from ordinary social restraints:

> Bending forward
> With stern faces,
> Pilgrims puff
> Up the steep bank
> In huge hats.
>
> Shouting I run
> In the other direction,

> Cheerful, unchaste,
> With open shirt
> And tinkling guitar. (64)

At a later, more disturbed stage, when they all fear that they are not loved, Emble and Quant, respectively, sing these stanzas:

> My mother weeps for me
> Who disappeared at play
> From home and hope like all who chase
> The blue elusive bird.
>
> Through gloomy woods I go
> Ex-demigod; the damp
> Awakes my wound; I want my tea
> But needed am of none. (91)

The severe abstraction of this technique is somewhat forbidding, for every new speech, as it were, rearranges the stage set. Every phrase, by its imagery and syntax, locates a feeling, and we must remain extraordinarily alert to tone in order to catch the nuances. On the other hand, Auden provides structural guidelines that make our path much easier than it ever is in Gertrude Stein's abstract work. For one thing, his plan of development, once we understand it, as we now can easily do with Callan's help, is precise and definite. At almost every phase all four characters experience parallel feelings, so that if one speech blurs for us, the next may make its significance clear. Besides, the accompanying narration tells us in plain prose just where we are and keeps us safely above the obscurest levels of mystification. And, finally, the general agreement among the characters to use a common imagery, that of landscape, gives the hard passages unity and makes simpler our task of seeing the connections between one realm and another, between the physical and social imagery and its psychological and moral meanings.

Thus the characters' quest for the truth about their own human position takes allegorical form through a Jungian landscape imagery which borrows as well from other parabolic forms that Auden admires: fairy tales, detective stories, childish fantasies, the dream-vision. The quest, in all its forms, is so attractive and hypnotic that we are ready to join and to follow the characters even through great obscurity. On the other hand, the allegorical journey through the psyche, the abstract landscape imagery, and the alliterative and stylized diction make quite impossible a too extensive identification with the characters. We may feel some question, even, as to whether the anti-Romantic machinery—"the pastoral convention in which a natural setting is contrasted with an artificial style of diction" (as the book jacket tells us) and the baroque extravagance to which Auden carries its refinements—does not overwhelm the reader; whether the insistence on attention to the riddles of the quest does not kill our sympathy for the questing figures. Many readers of poetry, after all, do not love word games. There are moments when the dramatic situation is conveyed in appropriately moving tones, particularly in some speches of Malin and Rosetta, but through most of the poem the high style characteristically filters out the feeling.

And yet this is not the whole story. Dr. Johnson felt the same way about "Lycidas," and the truth is that there is surely feeling in *The Age of Anxiety,* but it is managed differently from what we expect or usually like. Certainly 138 pages of cryptic alliterative verse is hard reading, and it is easy to be impatient with what seems in Auden an unscrupulous ingenuity. What we can admire, in spite of this impatience, is the workmanship; the verse is splendidly made. If the meter reminds us of Middle English, if the fantastic dream-journeys recall Dante and Langland, there is much to remind us also of Spenser: not only the pastoral allegory, the atmosphere of the quest, the whole half-childish world of fantasy, but also the unhurried delight in detail, the loving versification, the joy taken in the decorative. From any point of view that wants the reflection of human affairs in poetry to show a more immediate relation to current social and political urgencies, this new kind of verse, like Spenser's, inevitably seems an evasion—a disappearance into a rarefied atmosphere in which nothing matters but consonant values and metrical refinements. But, ornate as it is, the poem's subject is man and the two atlases, public and inner, in which he lives. The elaborate décor provides the setting for a highly stylized performance, but the drama is still that of the anxious human creature, its phases and variations caught and given form as in eighteenth-century fugues and sonatas.

Deft, witty, beautifully wrought, *The Age of Anxiety* certainly suggests that divine order whose "great coherences," according to Caliban in *The Sea and the Mirror*, art can only imperfectly mirror. If there seems too much of the order and too little humanity, still, as we study the poem more fully, we see more clearly how the actual human condition, with its clumsy component feelings, lies hidden in the beautiful crystals. Thus Malin's muted description of the "ruined rebel" in the hermetic gardens is really (among other possible readings) a picture of any man who, in a bright moment of earthly love, catches a glimpse of Paradise—that is, feels a radiance in the world around him:

> Tense on the parterre, he takes the hero's
> Leap into love; then, unlatching the wicket
> Gate he goes:
> The plains of his triumph appear empty,
> But now among their motionless
>
> Avenues and urns with extra élan
> Faster revolves the invisible corps
> Of pirouetting angels
> And a chronic chorus of cascades and birds
> Cuts loose in a wild cabaletta. (88)

Theatrical yet antirhetorical, carefully selecting the melodramatic detail yet depriving us of full melodramatic feeling and of the complacent rhyme, this discreet verse arranges for our pleasure a charming miniature; a pattern of inner feeling becomes a tiny ballet. Is it too discreet, too esoteric? It may not do for everyone; but it repays close study. From its rococo extreme, Auden's own later poems pull back in search of a truth more direct and warm in its speaking.

CHAPTER 16

Truth and Textures

A LTHOUGH little space remains to treat Auden's poems of the last twenty-five years, they lend themselves, luckily, to briefer discussion, not because they are inferior to the early poems, but because they are more of a piece. Auden's Christianity gave him a base for a style for his shorter poems. Mainly, I want to analyze this style as it appears throughout this period, and shall discuss only briefly, and later, the development from one of these volumes to the next: the new poems published in *Collected Poetry* and *Collected Shorter Poems* (1945 and 1950); those published in *Nones* (1951); in *The Shield of Achilles* (1955); in *Homage to Clio* (1960); and in *About the House* (1965).

I *The Everyday Hero*

Since Auden became a quieter poet in the 1940's, a poet of acceptance rather than of rebellion, most critics have not been kind. To the American Alfred Kazin his poetry seems "terribly impoverished in recent years";[1] to the British Philip Larkin he has become "an engaging, bookish, American talent, too verbose to be memorable and too intellectual to be moving."[2] If Auden is still a considerable influence on modern poetry (especially American), if everyone knows that he continues to produce work of admirable craftsmanship while his cohorts of the 1930's write less or less well, there is nevertheless a general suspicion of his elegance and of his chattiness—an impression that he has dribbled away his talent by not being serious enough. "Surely some dreadfully wrong-headed diffidence is here," writes Robert Mazzocco, "some waste, some evasion. It has always haunted me reading Auden's poems, and now, apparently, it haunts the poet himself. . . ."[3]

Such judgments seem to me entirely mistaken. Casual Auden's

poetry often is, but it is not trivial nor evasive. He himself excoriates those who think "that anyone who attempts to deal with things that matter must be a bore, that rather than run the risk of talking nonsense one should play it safe and stick to charming trifles."[4] But virtually the whole problem of the modern poem is that of erecting a poetic structure sufficiently ironic or oblique to permit "things that matter" to be treated without sentimentality or pretentiousness. What are these "things that matter"— Romantic passion, one's own emotional history, intense moments of identity with the cosmos? Mazzocco charges that "so much of his extraordinary complexity rests (can it be denied?) on the commonplace." Far from denying it, Auden would heartily agree. For him, as for Yeats, life rests on the ordinary; about it he builds his later poems—the familiar features of landscape ("Bucolics"), the hours of the day ("Horae Canonicae"), the rooms of a house ("Thanksgiving for a Habitat"). In the daily round can be read all the "things that matter"—intimations of death, God, the deepest patterns of human existence.

The truth about these patterns becomes increasingly important to Auden. Before his reader "is aware of any other qualities [a poem] may have, I want his reaction to be: 'That's true' or, better still, 'That's true: now, why didn't I think of it for myself?' To secure this effect I am prepared to sacrifice a great many poetic pleasures and excitements. . . . The ideal at which I aim is a style which shall combine the drab sober truthfulness of prose with a poetic uniqueness of expression. . . ."[5]

Since the truth about the patterns of ordinary human existence might make for a highly abstract poetry—the danger is always present—Auden usually presents the truth as it is experienced by someone. This method seems the only way in which the basically undramatic experience of an ordinary man can be presented dramatically. Auden quotes a doubtful Kierkegaard on this point: "If I would represent a hero who conquers kingdoms and lands, it can very well be represented in the moment, but a cross-bearer who every day takes up his cross cannot be represented either in poetry or in art, because the point is that he does it every day."[6] Always interested in what cannot be done, Auden does, in fact, represent in his poetry the man who every day takes up his cross.

That man is, of course, himself. In using his own experience as central, however, he takes particular care never to stress his gifts of insight, wit, and feeling, as a Romantic poet would do. He always implies that all men may have their points of merit, but that what he is concerned with in his poems are the respects in which most of them are equal: their possession of bodies and souls; their relationship to ordinary and fundamental needs, desires, satisfactions, disappointments.

The somberness of this description somewhat falsifies Auden's poems. They have their somber moments, but most of the memorable and ambitious poems are witty and casual in tone. The poet seems sometimes even garrulous as one subject recalls another and he chatters away like an imperturbable, benevolent, unstoppable raconteur. But this characteristic dramatic frame moves constantly between the surfaces and the depths of life, between the clear and the dark, the personal experience and the universal, the apparently trivial and its real meaning. Such oscillation is necessary because total seriousness in poetry is suspect; the ordinary poet's critical intelligence requires him to question all his most sacred truths and feelings. So the later poetry is full of statements that are serious but protected from both sentimentality and coldness by wit:

> The blessed will not care what angle they are
> > regarded from,
> Having nothing to hide. (*Nones,* 16)

> > After all, it's rather a privilege
> > amid the affluent traffic
> to serve this unpopular art which cannot be turned into
> > background noise for study
> or hung as a status trophy by rising executives. . . . (*House,** 10)

Such protective devices, multiplied on every side, form the basic structure of Auden's later poetry. His work has always used them, but now more than ever, and more consistently than ever. Now that his poetry is using himself as a feeling subject, it is essential to protect the work both from banality and egoism; this he achieves not only by mixing levels of seriousness and by presenting the elegant and witty speaker as flawed and ordinary in body and soul, but also by developing farther than ever before

---

About the House (New York, 1965).

those stylistic devices that, even from Auden's earliest poetry, had been suggestive of ambiguities and misgivings beneath a surface certainty.

The later poems are characterized, therefore, by the most extraordinary textures, which Auden creates mainly by his manipulation of syntax, tone color, and rhythms. His aim in doing so is always to surprise us, to attack our certainties with unexpectednesses, to resist the expected patterns of sentence structure, tone, and metrical regularity. But this resistance is not to pattern in general; depriving us of the old, he gives us new ones, new forms, to keep us alert, to stress the newness of the world and the inventiveness of poets, "that joy in beginning/for which our species was created." (*House*, 34)

II *Syntax, Tone, Rhythm*

Throughout Auden's career his command of English syntax is always astonishing. No other modern poet has such sovereignty over the syntactical possibilities of the language. Savoring his intricacies has on the admiring reader the same effect as reading late Henry James: after either experience, most other writing of the same genre seems pale and undistinguished. For Auden uses, it seems, every formula, every variation, the language has to offer, from the labyrinthine riddle—"What they were once was what they would not be;/Not liking what they are not is what now they are" (*Nones*, 52)—to the direct and choppy—"It hangs, it flogs, it fines, it goes. There is drink./There are wives to beat" (*Shield*, 26)—and the wayward, yet precisely articulated—

> So few of the Big
> Ever listen: that is why you have a great host
> Of superfluous screams to care for and
>
> Why, up and down like the Duke of Cumberland,
> Or round and round like the Laxey Wheel,
> The Short, The Bald, The Pious, The Stammerer went,
> As the children of Artemis go,
>
> Not yours. (*Clio,** 5)

---

*Homage to Clio (New York, 1960).

What is constant, even in the most meandering passages, is a crispness, a sharpness of outline, often achieved through parallel phrasing (as in all three examples above), that allows the syntax to get just as casual as it likes. For no matter how rambling the discourse, the sentence structure is almost always perfectly clear. Nevertheless, especially in the late poetry, it resists our expectations. We often expect a sentence to unfold in one way, only to have it turn in an unlooked-for direction. What appears to be the last noun in a series is actually the subject of the next verb:

> We know all about graphs
> and Darwin, enormous rooms no longer
> superhumanize, but earnest
>
> city planners are mistaken . . . (*House*, 6)

On first reading, too, I mistakenly expect the "but" to lead to a statement of what enormous rooms *do* do. Everywhere in these late poems we have to watch the syntax carefully, through all its snakelike twists.

If syntax has this ability to deceive us, to require alertness from us, so does the shifting tone. Central as never before, the tone keeps us jumping from one feeling to another, one frame of reference to another:

> The sin of Gluttony
> is ranked among the Deadly
> Seven, but in murder mysteries
> one can be sure the gourmet
> didn't do it. . . . (*House*, 25)

> When I disband from the world,
> and entrust my future to the Gospel Makers,
> I need not fear (not in neutral Austria) being called for
> in the waist of the night by deaf agents, never
> to be heard of on earth again. . . . (*House*, 33)

Here the poet's seriousness is protected from unbecoming egoism by the wit of "disband" and the ironic reference to literary critics; and it is both protected and deepened by the deliberately melodramatic allusion to the "deaf agents" who escort the protagonist of Kafka's *The Trial* to his death. Every phrase touches the subject with a different light, turns on it a different speech, yet all the speech seems one and whole. Auden seems really to be aiming at a verse equivalent of the rich changes in color and timbre that distinguish operatic voices. But the basis of this poetic fullness of tone is ordinary spoken English. Although the situations of these chatty poems are seldom precisely fixed enough to make them full dramatic monologues, the characteristic tones are basically those of casual conversation, not lyrical reflection. However highly ordered, however rhetorically complex, the sounds are those not of speeches but of speech.

Auden's rhythms, too, in these later poems, do several things at once—resist traditional metric pattern, establish new patterns, and reflect the range and movement of actual good talk. Experimental as always, he tries out many meters and verse forms: a canzone, sestinas, sonnets, haiku, clerihews, limericks, various intricate song forms, rime royal, heroic couplets; there is internal rhyme and apocopated rhyme; one of the most peculiar poems is "Dame Kind" (*Clio*), in a meter that mocks Browning's "A Grammarian's Funeral."

In general, despite their variety, these poems divide rhythmically into two groups—the metrical and the syllabic. Throughout his career, however, Auden's metrical poems have been of two kinds—those measured by the foot and those measured by the stress. The poems with strictly counted feet (those which tend to have a regular number of short syllables with each long one) are usually his more abstract or more obviously humorous pieces: sonnets, sestinas, jocular verses. But this category also includes a quietly personal poem like "New Year Letter" and some splendid heroic couplets. But from his earliest work his more sublime effects—the hawk's-eye imagery at its grandest, the large, prophetic tone—have been cast in a looser, accentual line, in which we count the stresses because the feet, though guided by a generally iambic or anapestic feeling, vary in the number of minor syllables.

We can find this pattern in very early poems—in *1928*, XVI, for example, where these lines are pentameter: "It is seen how excellent hands have turned to commonness./One, staring too long, went blind in a tower;/One sold all his manors to fight, broke through, and faltered." But Auden began very soon to carve a stanza out of such rough lines—in imitation of similar stanzas used in Greek and Latin poetry. Though he varies this stanza repeatedly and uses most of his variations only once, he develops one form that is almost standard for him—the quatrain whose first two lines are longer than the last two, and whose stress pattern, though varied much even within each poem, is most often 5-5-3-4 or 5-5-4-3. Examples in *Collected Poetry* are "Casino" (91), "As We Like It" (25-26), and "Journey to Iceland" (7-9). The poems on Spain, Dover, Oxford, schoolchildren, and "A Bride in the 30's" are all variations of the same metrical scheme. The flexible rhythm of all these pieces—I think of them as Alcaic because they recall that ancient four-line meter—helps them to achieve distance, elevation, ironic largeness:

> Without, the rivers flow among the wholly living,
> Quite near their trysts; and the mountains part them; and
> the bird
> Deep in the greens and moistures of summer
> Sings towards their work. (*CP*, 91)

This flexibility, the careless air with which each line meets its formal requirements (learned, no doubt, from Yeats), must have appealed to Auden as parabolic even of the human situation: man must be free to choose his Necessity. The language's normal rhythms struggle to evade the Necessity of the line-pattern, just as man struggles to avoid the knowledge and choices that alone can set him free. We need not push this kind of reasoning too far; it is enough to recognize Auden's interest in designs that combine regularity and looseness, surface disorder and underlying pattern. No wonder, then, that after he became acquainted in the 1930's with the quiet-toned syllabic poetry of Marianne Moore, he should investigate the possibilities of this new kind of patterning.

When did he begin? G. S. Fraser and Monroe Spears regard "Alonso to Ferdinand" in *The Sea and the Mirror* as Auden's first syllabic poem.[7] Blair points out that "Spring 1940" and "Autumn 1940" are earlier examples.[8] But Auden's first syllabics are to be found in "Crisis" and in his elegy on Freud, both works of 1939. These first attempts are still in the Alcaic form, but the measure is now one of syllable, not stress; both poems have a pattern of *11-11-9-10*, as do "Spring 1940" and "Autumn 1940."

144

As he worked over the form in the next few years (examples can be found in *CP*: 20-22, 45-46, 134, 441-42, 464), especially as he was seeking to rid his poetry of a too pretentious prophetic note and to center it in the ordinary life, he discovered the perfect suitability of syllabics to the poem expressive of quiet personal concern. The early syllabic poems are a bit stiff; still Alcaic in feeling, they have not arrived at a feeling of their own. But by the time of *The Sea and the Mirror*, Alonso's form has both dignity and personal warmth; and Prospero's long speech catches the tone of most of Auden's later syllabic poems—witty, self-critical, a bit garrulous, very human.

Many of the most memorable poems in the last four volumes are written in this important form—notably "In Praise of Limestone" and half the poems in the three sequences that dominate the later volumes—"Bucolics" and "Horae Canonicae" in *Shield*, and "Thanksgiving for a Habitat" in *House*. As Auden uses it, the syllabic verse has something of the same effect as the surprising syntax and changing tone color: one line may suggest one meter, but the next matching line will contradict it. Thus, "Homage to Clio" begins:

> Our hill has made its submission and the green
> Swept on into the north: around me,
> From morning to night, flowers duel incessantly,
> Color against color, in combats . . .

If these lines do not conclusively reject our stress-counting impulses (the syllable-pattern is *11-9-11-9*, adjacent vowels as in *flowers* and *duel* being counted as one), the next lines will. Again the point is to forestall the too complacent participation of the reader; it is also to suggest the extent of the speaker's casualness: no rigid meter for *his* talk, but a liquid flow of the language. Just as the syntax and the tone must never fall into obvious patterns, the syllables must never accidentally, for more than about a line, fall into some accentual pattern. The skill is in endlessly varying the design, the triple design of meter, sentence, and feeling.

But though the thought seems, from moment to moment, unkempt and formless, though the lines are hard for the ear to measure, we still do feel most of the lines as lines, feel an order in the palaver. This evident combination—*in the same words—*

145

of elegance and disorder, of control and laxity, has great power. Life, it seems to say, is at once form and process; the order develops out of the formlessness; the reflective meandering of chat, which, like life itself, rambling through all the dimensions of the trivial, does arrive somewhere at last—what else does it turn out to be but form?

III *Horace*

In a sense, the basic theme of all Auden's later books is this assertion. Despite the blur of ordinary life, everything makes sense; pattern is everywhere. We never see all of it, but nonetheless it is there. Ubiquitous parables show us, for all our troubles, how finely life is arranged. Auden's poetry does not slight its difficulties; social distress and personal anxiety are always central in his work. But where the early poetry arraigns and ridicules the guilty and the weak, and rebels against authority and tradition, the later work affirms even authority. The war between an irreconcilable We and They in which nothing would do for Them but total abolition has given way to a common human order of which We and They are alike indispensable members. The authorities, administrators, managers, Utopians—all temperamentally antipathetic to Auden—he recognizes as having their part to play (unsavory it may be, but his own is not blameless) in the working out of the world's form.

This reconciliation with the world (it is no accident that one of his finest works is based on *The Tempest*) is inevitably less exciting than the youthful stance of rebellion and challenge. Firmly classical, Auden's later poetry rejects most of the values attractive to energetic young readers—passion, revolt, defiance. On the other hand, its wisdom, its awareness of the sides of ordinary life, its balancing of multiplicities and unities, confusions and clarities, recommend it to seasoned readers. As the syllabic poems issue out of Latin meters, so Auden's poetry of the last twenty years has benefited from his long visits to Italy. Although the syllabic style may still owe something to Rilke and much to Marianne Moore, the intricate textures of these poems, their unpredictable formal progress, their sly development of balances and contrasts, are strongly reminiscent of Horace. Both poets are highly civilized and highly ironic; both know the country and the town but give us few details of their personal lives;

both have a strong sense of the limitations of life and the satisfactions of small pleasures; both want us to recognize what they tell us as true, as wise.

Nietzsche's description of Horace's poetry as "a mosaic of words" certainly fits Auden's, except that Auden does with phrases what Horace's language permits him to do with words—move them around into the most expressive order. And single words can balance whole phrases, as in Auden's remark to the shade of Louis MacNeice (my italics): "Though neither of our dads, like Horace's/*wiped his nose on his forearm,*/neither was *porphyry-born* . . ." (*House,* 9) One modern critic notes in Horace what is always in Auden, "the curious parallel existence of bold and tame, old and new." And, when we recall Auden's recent distaste for translatable imagery (see above, p. 109), it is startling to hear the same critic observe of Horace that "the sensitivity of expression which some poets achieved through an intuitive perception of unsuspected likeness [that is, striking imagery] is matched in Horace's lyric by experiments in the contrastive and combinatory potentialities of words."[9]

Horace, too, uses the casual excursus, the chatty parenthesis, the fanciful exaggeration, especially the witty suggestion that quite ordinary behavior owes something to the intervention of supernatural beings (in Auden: imps, demons, Dame Kind, Greek gods and goddesses). The structure of Horace's poems, as of Auden's, is often elusive and subtle; and the apparently irrelevant detail or digression comes only gradually to be seen as functional. He, too, seems to many readers a poet of the intellect rather than of feeling; but, although the outlook of both Horace and late Auden is generally sunny, each is capable of flaring out into quick bursts of feeling; and there is more feeling, anyway, in both poets, than one first thinks. Horace's poems often end without much flourish, with an almost antirhetorical flatness; Auden, in Horatian fashion, finishes many poems (like the one to MacNeice) quietly: ". . . dear Shade, for your elegy/ I should have been able to manage/something more like you than this egocentric monologue,/but accept it for friendship's sake." (*House,* 11) Finally, both poets are acute observers of people and of social and human patterns; and both discern the fundamental patterns and conflicts of life from within a framework of acceptance.

This poetry, then, requires time, leisure, maturity for its enjoyment. Retirement to the Sabine farm does not appeal to twenty or twenty-five, and even older readers sometimes think the quiet contemplation of life's follies and ironies to be politically irresponsible. Still, now that Western culture, like the Roman, has stirred the world with Romantic expectations of the impossible, there is much to be said for the poet who, beyond all the immediate and miscellaneous distress, can make out, quietly and elegantly, meanings that endure and fortify.[10]

IV *The Later Volumes*

Since the later volumes of Auden show less development than the earlier, the foregoing description can serve as a general guide to his shorter poems and sequences from 1941 to 1965. Nevertheless, the successive volumes do vary in quality and character, and a word should be said about each. In the early and middle 1940's Auden was busy with his impressive long poems; therefore, the new pieces in *Collected Poetry* (1945) are comparatively unambitious. I have already referred to the three poems in syllabics (20, 45, 134) and to the highly polished, cold and elegant stanzaic poems such as "Kairos and Logos" and "Canzone" (see p. 102). There are several metrical poems in a relaxed style that derives from the earlier Alcaic poems and leads to the later syllabic and accentual poems: "Mundus et Infans" and "At the Grave of Henry James."

Equally important is the poem in strict meter which is polished enough to be pleasing but also relaxed and somewhat (sometimes) personal in feeling—a genre that continues Auden's indebtedness to such poets as Frost, Robinson, Housman, Jonson. Such slight, graceful, but concentrated pieces rely largely on word-play, epigram, the neatness with which the thought is turned:

> Few as they are, these facts are all
> The richest moment can recall,
> However it may choose to group them,
> And, simple as they look, enough
> To make the most ingenious love
> Think twice of trying to escape them. (*CP*, 161)

All the subsequent volumes contain many such poems of low intensity but of elegant design and, often, of subtle idea. With the more deliberately casual poems that are usually syllabic, they form the bulk of Auden's later work.

Nones (1951) carries farther the development of these two main styles, the syllabic poems being especially numerous, various, and attractive. A highly experimental volume, *Nones* feels out new possibilities of arrangement, from blank-verse syllabics ("Not in Baedeker") to the highly operatic "The Duet." Several of the poems have an Italian setting, and Classical allusions begin to abound. If there is one series of ideas that can be read in most of the poems, it is something like this: The Just City, which all of us would like to see exist, depends mainly on the conduct of our inner lives, on loving God and our neighbor instead of ourselves. To bring about such a condition requires us to make the best use of the gifts we have and of our immediate situations, not to expect too much of life or of ourselves. We can also distinguish here and there between what is truly valuable and what is only apparently so; we can try to see the meanings that underlie the surfaces of life; and we can *"Bless what there is for being."* (79)

The Shield of Achilles (1955) is much less miscellaneous than *Nones*. It begins with the seven-poem sequence "Bucolics" and, after fourteen other pieces, ends with the seven-poem sequence "Horae Canonicae." These very impressive sequences are beautifully constructed out of poems in various forms; finely wrought, rich in texture, they move continually from one mood or tone to another. Both try to see what realities lie below ordinary surfaces we do not usually subject to such penetrating scrutiny. To the water in streams, for example, Auden says, you

> still talk to yourself: nowhere are you disliked;
> Arching your torso, you dive from a basalt sill,
> Canter across white chalk, slog forward
> Through red marls, the aboriginal pilgrim,
>
> At home in all sections, but for whom we should be
> Idolaters of a single rock, kept apart
> By our landscapes, excluding as alien
> The tales and diets of all other strata. (28)

Nor is this talk merely idle and ingenious: streams, like everything else, are parables and show man things about himself. This volume, too, contains, outside the sequences, a few poems that are surely masterpieces: "The Shield of Achilles," " 'The Truest

149

Poetry Is the Most Feigning,'" and "The Willow-Wren and the Stare." Auden's poetry achieves in this book a classical order and beauty marred only by an occasional blandness or archness—in the flat "Epitaph for the Unknown Soldier," for example; or in sly references to some loved one: "while, near enough, a real darling/Is cooking a delicious lunch." (19)

A major theme in all these volumes (and in all Auden's poetry) but one that receives special emphasis in *Homage to Clio* (1960) is the opposition between History and Nature. Nature, represented by Dame Kind and by "the appetitive goddesses" Aphrodite and Artemis, governs animals, plants, kings, warriors, and fleshly lovers; though important in human life, it lacks final point, for it offers imperatives, not choices. An organism is driven to act as it does; it does not decide. Clio, on the other hand, the Muse of History, is, more precisely, "Muse of the unique/Historical fact." In short, what makes a man fully human is his involvement in the actual details of ordinary living. The great conquerors matter less than "those who bred them better horses,/Found answers to their questions, made their things,/Even those fulsome/Bards they boarded. . . ." (23)

Not the natural drives, then, but an interest in them, a thirst to understand and manipulate nature, begins to make human beings historical, sets them in a world of moral choices. "The significant difference" between men and animals "is not that man has speech, but that he talks to himself, not that he has reason, but that he reasons about reasoning."[11] On the other hand, still loyal to Kierkegaard's leap and even Homer Lane's love, Auden continues to insist that reason, planning, purpose may be less effective guides to a man's best life than instinct or luck. The road to that life is "Unlookable for, by logic, by guess:/Yet some strike it, and are struck fearless." (62) Mistakes have their uses. History and Nature together make man what he is.

If *Homage to Clio* is less rich stylistically than *The Shield of Achilles,* it has its brilliant moments. It also has more fun: the poet writes limericks and clerihews, and celebrates bathtubs and kitchens. But, as to whether or not serious poems can be written on such subjects, Auden himself, in 1955, is skeptical: "There are some products of technology—kitchen refrigerators, for example—which seem to me an unqualified good; but however grateful I may feel towards mine at cocktail time, I cannot see myself writing a panegyric ode to it as I could have written

centuries ago to a king who at his marriage ordered wine to flow from the public fountains."[12]

Auden goes on to say that the modern poet "can only produce genuine work about events to which he has a personal relation"; yet if he risked more, "he would find that the possible area of the personal is larger than he supposes." When the impressive prose piece, "Dichtung und Wahrheit," in *Homage to Clio,* doubts the feasibility of writting a good personal love poem, it is really raising the broader question of whether any intensely personal poem can be written. It decides not. But the latest work of Auden seeks, through the mannered and witty treatment of physical surroundings, to move ever closer to the poet himself in order to show him, an example of man, as fully and meaningfully involved in Nature and History.

His most recent volume, *About the House* (1965), is richly personal. He writes not only of kitchens but of all the rooms in his Austrian house, even the water closet (a hilarious poem). And, as he writes with disarming casualness of his intimate connections with rooms, his more personal affections slip in; his feelings for his friends are more openly stated than ever before, not directly but in poems ostensibly about something else. Postscripts, haiku, transliterations, slight occasional poems—all give us the sense of a man engaged in verbal experiments: poetry is the milieu of this particular creature, the thing he does that makes him historical, as other men create coins or weapons or music.

Careful always to avoid Romantic egoism, Auden again makes no claims for this speaker's moral valor: he is weak, flawed, not a great villain (to claim that would be equally Romantic); he is merely an ordinary sinner. But he *is* an artist; he has written fine poems, possibly just *because* of the yielding to temptation that in the moral sphere is deplorable. So he can think of no worse nor more fitting punishment for an artist than that God should set him, on Judgment Day, to "reciting by heart/the poems you would/have written, had/your life been good." (13)[13] We find, altogether, in these poems, an impressive picture of an ordinary man, one fully committed to living, working, loving, and, finally, praising in an age of anxiety, and even in ignorance: "about/ catastrophe or how to behave in one/I know nothing, except what everyone knows—/if there when Grace dances, I should dance." (84)

CHAPTER 17

Critical, Operatic, Inconclusive

POETRY is only one of Auden's careers. Teacher, critic, playwright, translator, librettist, he is a remarkably versatile man of letters, as active and energetic as the Goethe whose *Italian Journey* he has helped to translate and whose career he sees in a recent poem as parallel with his own: "I should like to become, if possible,/a minor atlantic Goethe. . . ." (*House*, 10) Although Auden does not dominate his age's culture as Goethe did, the breadth of his interests and activities gives some substance to the claim. In the last two decades his libretti and his criticism especially have been marked with distinction. These genres, however, raise large questions that this study can discuss only briefly.

As for the criticism, I have already indicated that Auden's early essays and reviews, though often provocative, are commonly insistent and strident in tone. In accord with the more relaxed manner of all his later work, the essays of the last two decades are almost always charming, genial, richly suggestive, and modest. The great strength of his critical intelligence is in making distinctions and in pursuing them farther than anyone else would believe possible or useful. This exercise is often a fascinating one and can result in such extraordinary assertions as that (each the last step in quite convincing arguments) Falstaff is emblematic of Christian charity, or Iago of modern science. Auden's first volume of criticism *The Enchafèd Flood, or The Romantic Iconography of the Sea* (1950) systematically pursues Romantic literature through all its sea imagery. His observations are often enlightening and probably valid, but the book is tiresomely single-minded and the distinctions wearying. The author seems more bent on his game of equivalences and significations than the subject appears to justify. But his incidental essays are usually far more agreeable, and his collection of many of his

152

best in *The Dyer's Hand* (1962) makes one of the most readable, witty, perceptive, and profound critical books of the century.

In particular, his ability to ferret out the parable hidden in every literary or actual situation; his insight into perspectives of all kinds—fantasy, science, or subjective experience—and his awareness of them as sometimes opposed, sometimes complementary, sometimes interdependent; his power of thinking himself into any point of view and developing all its moral and intellectual tendencies to their logical conclusions—these gifts are not merely instructive, they are almost terrifying. In a century dominated very largely by psychoanalytic inquiry, political fairy tales, the middle-class search for roles and stances, Auden both as a poet and a critic is the man who, more than any other, is determined to show us—obliquely or directly—what we are *really* doing, what our wishes, our actions, our values *really* mean. Even where we feel he may not be right, his procedure has a frightening clarity which warns us that if total truth is not precisely here, it is not far off; that this is, indeed, the way in which the human contraption works, through emblems and allegories, myths and habits; that every social and personal structure conceals and expresses some truth about its anxious makers.

Auden's activity in translating and writing opera libretti has occupied him considerably in the last twenty years—so much so that since 1947, except for his poem sequences, all his longer works have been libretti. He and Chester Kallman have translated Mozart's *The Magic Flute* and *Don Giovanni*, and Karl Ditters von Dittersdorf's *Arcifanfano, King of Fools*. After Auden had worked alone on the libretto for Benjamin Britten's opera *Paul Bunyan* (1941), he and Kallman collaborated on the libretti for Stravinsky's *The Rake's Progress* (1951); for the one-act *Delia or a Masque of Night* (1953), which still awaits its music; for Hans Werner Henze's *Elegy for Young Lovers* (1961); and for Henze's *The Bassarids* (1966). Since these works are only partly Auden's, partly his collaborator's, partly the composer's, and (with translations) partly the original librettist's, and especially since I have never seen any performance of the operas for which Auden and Kallman wrote libretti, it seems wise not to discuss these works in detail as representative of Auden's art.

A word or two, however, will suggest the connection of these

153

works with Auden's other poetry. As we might expect, the operas are allegorical fables, presented with deliberate artifice; and their themes are common ones in Auden's later poetry: the necessity to make choices guided by Love, the difference between Life and Art. In writing for a composer, the librettists inevitably sacrifice some of the richness of verbal texture that Auden's poetry usually has; but even though the verse is too often bland, the moral problems are nicely posed, the apparently simple verse is sometimes weighted with considerable meaning, occasional scenes are richer in suggestion, verbally denser and more subtle than we usually think possible in opera, and something of Auden's complex virtuosity is conveyed by the elegant pageantry.[1]

The very fact that Auden has chosen this kind of work indicates to what extent he has rejected Romantic egoism. Writing libretti (not to speak of translating them) requires a poet to subordinate his own personality to that of the composer's, his own art to music. Indeed, Auden's whole career exhibits a talent for collaboration unprecedented in any important English writer since the Jacobean dramatists. He has collaborated not only on translations and libretti but on travel books, poems, plays, textbooks, anthologies, films, and a pamphlet on education. There is nothing aloof about this poet; Auden is a man who takes part, who participates actively in the common literary life.

Even his conversion to Christianity and his repudiation of secular humanism do not in any sense represent a withdrawal from responsibility, as critics have often unfairly charged. On the contrary, no fine writer of the twentieth century has been so sensitive to its intellectual currents, so ready to try on hats, to grant a hearing to every claimant, and to do so with sympathy and yet with discrimination. Perhaps because he is so fully of our time, so deeply involved in it, so quietly yet unmistakably an influence on it, we have tended to take for granted his wit, his elegance, his art, and his insight.

Yet Auden's involvement seems especially valuable because it is balanced by his detachment—his insistence on seeing the immediate moment (which includes his own feeling and action) from a distance, from estranging and therefore illuminating perspectives. Critics who complain of his lack of commitment are usually unsympathetic to what he is committed to. The deepest things to which important writers are committed are not often political causes or religious doctrines; their loyalties are rather

154

to certain ways of thinking and feeling—to *patterns* of commitment, of hesitation, of active or passive acceptance or denial. If our own commitment to an author is to anything less deep in him than this, if it is merely to his Anglicanism or his Marxism, it may not survive the next doctrinal debate.

Thus Auden—despite his devotion to Freud and Marx, the Christian poems which occasionally seem too positive and knowing, the arrogant tone of his early essays and the assured categorical distinctions of the later ones—is fundamentally a poet of doubt, of uncertainty, of insecurity, of hesitations, second thoughts, qualifications—in short, of anxiety. In an age when nothing is clear, all the certitudes gone, perhaps the best we can do is to lunge after one idea or another, to embrace some orthodoxy, to make the leap of faith. The extravagance, the frequency, of Auden's leaps confirm the undercurrent of worry beneath even the tones of joy. So, from time to time, he finds a sage (Freud, Marx, Kierkegaard) or a career (teaching, film work, free-lance writing) or a new literary form, or a new country, a new church, a new home for spring and summer. What makes all this turning and turning most impressive poetically is that it is all done in the open: there is no hiding the doubts and hesitations, the other thoughts.

This anxiety, which is only intensified by the early poetry's tones of total certainty, even reaches at times to a fear that there will be no meaning, no intercourse between realms of being. Such intercourse—between parts of our lives, between people, between God and man, abstract and concrete, meaning and object—is what chiefly validates experience, the Incarnation that wakes the Sleeping Beauty, Life. In Auden's poetry the one intolerable possibility that is not often looked at as such, but which provides the unspoken source of all its anxieties, is that such intercourse will stop, or that it is only an illusion. The nightmare basic to his work is not that the world is evil but that it is meaningless. If Tennyson is, as Auden says, "the great English poet of the Nursery," who must constantly assure himself of his own identity,[2] Auden's work seems rooted in a similar primal fear—that of losing touch, of being really alone. Freud, Marx, Christ in turn give hope of recharging a dead world— imaged successively in glaciers and abandoned mines, in the blank physical surfaces of a decadent society, in the trivial joys, despairs, and insights of a prosperous one.

The problem of an Auden poem, from this point of view, is to certify reality, and the technique for doing this is fundamentally Jamesian: truth (that benevolent classical light to which we can be led only by Romantic processes of derangement) illuminates the world and, by showing us its patterns filled with moral significance, redeems it from unmeaning. Poetry affirms this process and, through this process, life itself.

In Auden's later years (especially after 1950), the need to be sure that the world is really substantial seems much less desperate. By the time his religious faith has become habitual, he seems more assured that everything really *is*: faith in God for Auden is largely faith that things exist, for things exist only when they exist meaningfully. I have suggested that Auden's later poetry has a wise complexity, quite grand in its way, but what many readers feel as comparatively unexciting in it is, I think, that it has passed through, has survived, and no longer therefore fully expresses this terrifying anxiety as to whether the world, or *anything*, is really there. What this poetry does remain expressive of is the high perspective and the broad sympathies of a man who has come through decades of feeling such anxiety and of seeing it all around him, and who knows and can tell us the value of everything in a world now assuredly real but still filled with real anxieties.

One irony of this development is worth noting. The early poems often show an arrogance of manner, a certainty of tone, so exaggerated as to contribute to Auden's general portrait of our anxiety and desperation, just as Kafka's narrative style, with its meticulous emphasis on physical fact, contributes to his picture of a world where one can be sure of nothing. In later years, though his work is as precise as ever, Auden's tone and manner are more modest, his confession of weakness more honest and simple. The irony is that critics have interpreted this loss of bluster as a loss of personal confidence—as a sign that Auden now sees he has wasted his talent. Precisely the opposite is probably true; it is only the man who has become strong (even Truly Strong) who can afford to speak with such honest regret.

Some of Auden's early techniques he has discarded along the way; some he has taken with him. The banal phrase, the casual style, the hawk's-eye vision survive in one form or another, but he has stripped his work of the unintentional overtone, the vague reverberation, on which Romantic poetry too often rests its appeal. In general, we can say that in resisting the art of the rhapsode he has developed two principal methods. The less remarkable is the direct, objective explanation of truth, using traditional figures such as personification, hyperbole, amplification; but the abstraction of this technique limits its largeness.

The second method is to present the truth more dramatically, as something desired, pursued, and perhaps achieved by someone whose unfolding feeling is the basic design of the poem. All his early work in parody, in establishing his myth of rebellion and exile, in constructing the situations out of which the speakers of his songs and ballads emerge, taught him much about the subtleties of having a flawed dramatic character tell the truth. His best poems can be seen as experiments in balancing the perception with the perceiver, in achieving between them a classical poise that mediates between the human reader and the impersonal truth. His poetry learns to be instructive without being didactic, personal but not Romantic; what it means it often says indirectly, through ironic frames, but it says, on the whole, no more than it means. It gives us allegorical designs to figure out, and memorable words to repeat, but Auden scrupulously refuses to lure our vaguest emotions into the service of his own sacred beings or events.

Central and crucial in his work is the opposition between enchantment and disenchantment. In a sense, he hardly writes of anything else. The distinctions between Art and Life, the frequent combination of hope and skepticism, the techniques of ironic perspective—all dramatize an attitude that recognizes both the charm of magic and illusion ("the delicious lie") and the superiority of goodness and truth. Auden's poetry explores finely and without sentimentality the pathos (even at times the evil) of those who, living in one world, try to escape into another. Still, all such wish is not bad: it foreshadows the divine, it rescues us from the untruth of mere fact, it suggests varieties of action and feeling that we need to live in the light of. The problem is to reconcile enchantment with disenchantment, Art with Life, to know which is which, and when each (or a union of both) is appropriate.

Through all his work runs a basic fable and a basic character: man as a lucky and gifted third son whose quest for meaningful life can succeed only if he discovers its paradoxical key. Being lucky is necessary, but it is not enough. It is not enough, either, to work out the answer by careful study and logic; for life, however logical in its structures here and there, in its deepest currents defies logic, is all trapdoors, sudden darknesses, exceptions. Seeing this, the third son recognizes his limitations, submits to the conditions of his existence, and in the very act of submission (which must, however, be repeated for the rest of his life) achieves the object of his quest: continuous existence. For the basic condition to which he has submitted, though it looks like defeat and death, turns out to be love.

How good is Auden's poetry? How long will people read it? No one, of course, is in a position to say. Comparison with Yeats and Eliot is inevitably misleading, for in our judgments of greatness in poetry we still use Romantic standards. When we speak of Yeats as greater than Eliot, and of both as greater than Auden, we still have some notion, even as we ridicule Arnold, that greatness involves grandeur. The poets we think of as great are all grand—Homer, Dante, Shakespeare, Milton; and although we have finally managed to include Chaucer sometimes in such lists, it is mainly because he has been dead so long. What we still want from contemporary poets is uplift, moments of exaltation and wonder, a feeling that life is lofty and rich. The canny poet, like Horace, Chaucer, Dryden, or Auden, seems to be operating on a different level. His usual subject is not the heroic and the transcendental but the normally human, and he achieves depth by other means than reverberating symbols and resonant tones.

As critics study Auden more fully in years to come, I suspect we shall see more clearly not only his psychological penetration but the force of his delicate poetic strategies, his superb balances, his unprecedented uses of the comic, his careful arrangements of surprises that disturb our expectations and yet fulfill them, the harmonies that are at once resolved and disconcerting. He disconcerts us so oddly that we think he must be at fault. We have hardly any previous experience with literary irony pushed so far, made to do so many things, in single poems and throughout a long career. But we ought by now to guess that the reason a poet like Auden puzzles is that we have not yet understood him and to think it likely, as in similar past cases, that as the world we live in grows clearer to us, these intricate ironies will seem more and more appropriate to it. Has a poet as complex and skillful as Auden ever been less than great? And there is more to come.

Notes and References

Chapter One

1. Randall Jarrell, "Changes of Attitude and Rhetoric in Auden's Poetry," *Southern Review*, VII (Autumn, 1941), 326-49.
2. Christopher Isherwood, *Lions and Shadows* (New York, 1947).
3. "Henry James and the Artist in America," *Harper's*, CXCVII (July, 1948), 40.

Chapter Two

1. Monroe Spears, *The Poetry of W. H. Auden: The Disenchanted Island* (New York, 1963), p. 3.
2. "As It Seemed to Us," *New Yorker*, XLI (April 3, 1965), 169-70.
3. Spears, p. 13.
4. Stephen Spender, *World Within World* (New York, 1951), p. 46.
5. "As It Seemed to Us," p. 178.
6. C. Day Lewis, *The Buried Day* (London, 1960), p. 176.
7. Spears, pp. 82-83.
8. Carlo Izzo, "The Poetry of W. H. Auden," in Spears, ed., *Auden* (Englewood Cliffs, 1964), p. 127.
9. See, for example, the caricatures of such guardians in *The Dog Beneath the Skin* and *The Ascent of F6*.
10. "As It Seemed to Us," p. 180.
11. See Justin Replogle's "The Gang Myth in Auden's Early Poetry," *Journal of English and Germanic Philology*, LXI (1962), 481-95.
12. *The Orators* (London, 1932), p. 14.

Chapter Three

1. Barbara Everett, *Auden* (Edinburgh, 1964), pp. 25-27. Her whole discussion of the ambivalences of the early verse is illuminating.
2. See Groddeck's *Das Buch vom Es* (1923), translated as *The Book of the It* (London, 1949; New York, 1961).
3. Homer Lane, *Talks to Parents and Teachers* (London, 1928), p. 177.
4. *The Age of Anxiety* (New York, 1947), p. 134.

Chapter Four

1. This is why I have not adopted Monroe Spears' picturesque term, "the Nordic mask" (*The Poetry of W. H. Auden*, p. 22), to describe these poems. To me, what distinguishes them from others is their imagery, not the Norse landscape and not even the Old English style. In Spears' classification (see Note 7, below) the poems of war that lack the landscape or the alliterative devices have to be moved into some other category even when their texture, along with the oracular, elliptical manner, links them to the Norse poems in feeling. Anyway, since every poem combines the several elements of the style in a different way, its limits should not be set too strictly.

2. Everett, p. 22.

3. A fair example is F. W. Cook's "Primordial Auden," *Essays in Criticism*, XII (Oct., 1962), 402-12. Cook analyzes the 1928 *Paid on Both Sides* as a Marxist piece.

4. See Replogle's "Social Philosophy in Auden's Early Poetry," *Criticism*, II (Fall, 1960), 351-61; and his "Auden's Marxism," *PMLA*, LXXX (Dec., 1965), 584-95.

5. Everett, pp. 20-21.

6. See Auden's review of *The Complete Works of John Skelton*, ed. Philip Henderson, in *Criterion*, XI (Jan., 1932), 316-19.

7. It is useful to know Spears' names for six styles he distinguishes in the early poems (22-27; 34-35): the Nordic mask (see Note 1, above); "the clipped lyric"—that is, the elliptical poem in Skeltonic style; the middle or colloquial style, in casual and easy English; a high style ("florid, extravagant, elevated, profuse; usually it is written in long lines, and it often exhibits baroque incongruities of diction" [25] and aims at mock-heroic effects); "the Rilkean sonnet"; and the popular style in which "the trite and flat language of popular songs and speech is used for satirical effect, and the poem is spoken by a *persona*" (34-35).

8. See the Preface to *CP* (1945); and the Foreword to the revised edition of *The Orators* (1966).

9. Spears reads it differently (47-48).

10. Stephen Spender, *The Destructive Element: A Study of Modern Writers and Beliefs* (London, 1935), p. 268.

11. "Honour," in *The Old School: Essays by Divers Hands*, ed. Graham Greene (London, 1934), p. 17.

12. Any student of *The Orators* should consult two recent articles which have appeared since my text was completed: W. H. Sellers, "New Light on Auden's *The Orators*," *PMLA*, LXXXII (Oct., 1967), 455-64; and Edward Mendelson, "The Coherence of Auden's *The Orators*," *ELH*, XXXV (March, 1968), 114-33.

Notes and References

Chapter Five

1. See, for example, "Mimesis and Allegory," *English Institute Annual,* 1940, ed. Rudolf Kirk (New York, 1941), pp. 1-19. A relevant quotation from this essay appears below on p. 96.
2. "A Literary Transference," *Southern Review,* VI (Summer, 1940), 83-84.
3. Review in *Criterion,* XII (Jan., 1933), 289.
4. Replogle, "Auden's Marxism" (See Note 4 to Chapter Four).
5. Introduction to *The Poet's Tongue* (London, 1935), x. See this introduction, *passim,* and the essay listed in Note 8, below.
6. See Spears, p. 86.
7. Spears, p. 86.
8. "Psychology and Art," *The Arts To-day,* ed. Geoffrey Grigson (London, 1935), p. 19.
9. John G. Blair, *The Poetic Art of W. H. Auden* (Princeton, 1965).

Chapter Six

1. *New Country,* ed. Michael Roberts (London, 1933), p. 199.
2. But see Replogle's "Auden's Marxism," esp. 585-86, for the best study of this play, which he sees as mainly non-Marxist. Note that "New Year Letter" shows Auden at a later stage between two views of life, just in the process of changing.
3. *The Dance of Death* (London, 1933), p. 16.
4. As for the terrible blank-verse exchange between Ransom and his mother, it is hard to believe Auden wrote it—or that he did *not* write Ransom's splendid opening prose speech.

Chapter Seven

1. *New Country,* p. 207.
2. In *CP* (38) and *Collected Shorter Poems 1930-1944* (London, 1950) "moneybug" is misprinted "moneybag."
3. *Letters from Iceland* (New York, 1937), p. 21. Copyright 1937, 1965 by W. H. Auden and Louis MacNeice.
4. For this term, and for some of the ensuing discussion, I am indebted to Dr. Leslie Palmer.

Chapter Eight

1. See Blair, pp. 130-34; Spears, pp. 110-12; Cleanth Brooks and Robert Penn Warren, *Understanding Poetry,* 3d. ed. (New York,

1960), pp. 332-35; Edward C. McAleer, "As Auden Walked Out," *College English*, XVIII (Feb., 1957), 271-72.

2. See, for example, *Poets of the English Language*, ed. Auden and Norman Holmes Pearson (London, 1952), esp. Auden's Introduction to Vol. III (xv) and to Vols. IV and V (*passim*).

3. *New Republic*, CIII (Nov. 25, 1940), 716.

4. In *Best Broadcasts of 1939-40*, ed. Max Wylie (New York, 1940), p. 37.

Chapter Nine

1. *Journey to a War* (New York, 1939), p. 301. In *CP* the last lines are altered to fit Auden's newly acquired Christian viewpoint.

2. Criticism has evidently made Auden sensitive about the weaknesses of his early poems, and he has revised frequently, deleting *the* wherever he can and avoiding multiple conjunctions. Where the corrections improve poems that suffered from hasty composition (forced rhymes or idle chatter), the critic can only applaud. But it seems a pity to destroy the unique and impressive texture of poems like "In Time of War" by wholesale changes made from a later, unsympathetic point of view. Yeats's later revisions of early poems almost always improved them; Auden's do not. And it is melancholy to see a splendid line like "Some people have been happy; there have been great men" (which conveys so finely the speaker's desperate wish to convince himself [*CP*, 325]) give way to the flat "Some have been happy; some, even, were great men" (*Collected Shorter Poems, 1927-1957*, p. 133). One wishes Auden would leave his past alone.

Chapter Ten

1. "Living Philosophies: VII. Morality in an Age of Change," *Nation*, CXLVII (Dec. 24, 1938), 691.

2. "Rilke in English," *New Republic*, C (Sept. 6, 1939), 135.

3. "A Great Democrat," *Nation*, CXLVIII (March 25, 1939), 352.

4. "Tradition and Value," *New Republic*, CII (Jan. 15, 1940), 90.

5. See "Jacob and the Angel," *New Republic*, CI (Dec. 27, 1939), 292-93.

6. "Eros and Agape," *Nation*, CLII (June 28, 1941), 757.

7. "A Note on Order," *Nation*, CLII (Feb. 1, 1941), 132.

8. "Eros and Agape," 756. The next four quotations are also taken from this essay.

9. "Tradition and Value," 90.

10. Spears, "The Dominant Symbols of Auden's Poetry," *Sewanee Review*, LIX (Summer, 1951), 413.

11. Ed. James A. Pike (London, 1956), pp. 31-43. Two quotations that follow cite page numbers from this book.

12. Introduction to *The Living Thoughts of Kierkegaard* (New York, 1952), p. 13.

13. *Ibid.*, p. 14.

14. *Ibid.*, p. 16.

15. The term Agape he draws mainly from the influential book of the 1930's, Anders Nygren's *Agape and Eros: A Study of the Christian Idea of Love* (London, 1932), and from the later, popular *Love and the Western World,* by Denis de Rougemont, which Auden reviews in the above-cited essay, "Eros and Agape."

16. "Mimesis and Allegory," *English Institute Annual,* 1940 ed. Rudolf Kirk (New York, 1941), pp. 18-19.

Chapter Eleven

1. It ought to be noted that a few of the discursive poems in *OTI* have this remote bleakness of outlook—"Casino" and "Epilogue." These chronological layers overlap; the powerful harmonies coexist with the toneless despair. But then the harmonies subside for a while or are pressed into the service of severely ironic ballads, while the deadly despair continues. On Dante, see "New Year Letter," *CP*, 269-70.

2. *Cf.* "A Great Democrat," cited above in Note 3 to Chapter Ten. This review of a book on Voltaire is relevant to both the Voltaire and the Pascal poems.

3. *Another Time* was published Feb. 7, 1940, according to Bloomfield.

Chapter Twelve

1. Rainer Maria Rilke, *Duino Elegies,* tr. J. B. Leishman and Stephen Spender (New York, 1939), pp. 37, 39. Auden's review of this volume is listed in the next note.

2. "Rilke in English," *New Republic,* C (Sept. 6, 1939), 135.

3. Isherwood, "Some Notes on Auden's Poetry," *New Verse,* No. 26-27 (Nov., 1937), 4.

4. *The Contemporary Poet As Artist and Critic,* ed. Anthony Ostroff (Boston, 1964), p. 186.

5. Blair, esp. Chapters II and III.

6. Blair's book is excellent in its description of Auden's devices for achieving generality. At the same time, it seems to me to err somewhat in depicting Auden as too much the calculating strategist. Blair himself acknowledges this (193). But not only does the unconscious contribute a good deal to the working out of an Auden poem; the

poetry very largely speaks of, and dramatizes, the impingement of unconscious and irrational forces on ordinary conscious life. The id, the It, the spectre of Caliban, the "gibbering fist-clenched creature" (*CP*, 387), "the dark thing you could never abide to be with" (*CP*, 390), is always present or virtually present, and so is Grace, God, the Unconditional: meaning always lurks in the shadows, is seen through "chinks of the forest," stands ready to invest ordinary things with life. Auden's severe hostility to Romanticism, after all, confesses some Romantic impulses. In concentrating so much on Auden's method, which, since no one had really spotted it before, needed to be analyzed, Blair somewhat slights and misrepresents the thematic material. And since both form and theme work together, Blair's description of Auden's strategies sometimes seems more simple than they are, as if Auden were merely showing us a drawing of lines and shapes that cross, instead of presenting dramatically whole realms of discourse and apprehension suddenly or secretly invaded and transformed by other, deeper, and more dreadful realms.

Chapter Thirteen

1. See Callan's articles referred to below in Note 1 to Chapter Fourteen, and in Notes 3, 5, and 6 to Chapter Fifteen.
2. Lane, *Talks to Parents and Teachers*, p. 177.

Chapter Fourteen

1. Edward Callan, "Auden's *New Year Letter*: A New Style of Architecture," *Renascence*, XVI (1963), 13-19, reprinted in Spears' *Auden*, pp. 152-59.
2. Charles Williams, *The Descent of the Dove* (London, 1963), p. 176. The Montaigne passage appears on p. 175.

Chapter Fifteen

1. Blair, p. 106.
2. This chapter tries mainly to suggest the general nature and value of these complex works. Anyone studying them closely can find valuable analyses of their philosophical structure and image-patterns in the essays cited below.
3. Edward Callan, "Auden and Kierkegaard: The Artistic Framework of *For the Time Being*," *Christian Scholar*, XLVIII (Fall, 1965), 211-23.

4. G. S. Fraser has criticized this passage as snobbish along somewhat different lines. See Spears, ed., *Auden*, pp. 90-91.

5. Callan, "Auden's *New Year Letter . . .*" I quote from Spears' *Auden*, p. 159. See also Callan's longer study of *The Sea and the Mirror* in "Auden's Ironic Masquerade: Criticism as Morality Play," *University of Toronto Quarterly*, XXXV (Jan., 1966), 133-43; Blair's discussion, pp. 106-17; Justin Replogle, "Auden's Religious Leap," *Wisconsin Studies in Contemporary Literature*, VII (Winter-Spring, 1966), 47-76; and Lee M. Whitehead, "Art as Communion: Auden's 'The Sea and the Mirror'," *Perspective*, XIV (Spring, 1966), 171-78.

6. Callan, "Allegory in Auden's *The Age of Anxiety*," *Twentieth Century Literature*, X (Jan., 1965), 155-65.

Chapter Sixteen

1. Alfred Kazin, "The Function of Criticism Today," *Commentary*, XXX (Nov., 1960), 104.

2. Philip Larkin, "What's Become of Wystan?" *Spectator*, No. 6890 (July 15, 1960), 104.

3. Robert Mazzocco, "The Poet at Home," *New York Review*, V (Aug. 5, 1965), 7.

4. "One of the Family," *New Yorker*, XLI (Oct. 23, 1965), 242.

5. *The Contemporary Poet As Artist and Critic*, pp. 185-86 (see Note 4 to Chapter Twelve).

6. "A Preface to Kierkegaard," *New Republic*, CX (May 15, 1944), 686.

7. Spears, p. 248, note 43.

8. Blair, pp. 150-51, note 50.

9. N. E. Collinge, *The Structure of Horace's Odes* (London, 1961), pp. 13, 19. See also Steele Commager, *The Odes of Horace* (New Haven, 1962).

10. Much still remains to be said about the influence on Auden throughout his career not only of Horace but of Roman or Classical poetry in general. *Cf.* his interest in epigrams, epitaphs, tributes, and the genre of the occasional poem.

11. "The Dyer's Hand," Part I, *Listener*, LIII (June 16, 1955), 1066.

12. "The Dyer's Hand," Part III, *Listener*, LIII (June 30, 1955), 1152.

13. Mazzocco (see p. 138 and Note 3 above) misreads this poem, thinking that Auden is saying his poems would have been *better* if his life had been better. *Cf. Elegy for Young Lovers*, where precisely the same point is the opera's main theme.

Chapter Seventeen

1. Blair has an excellent essay on *The Rake's Progress* (154-84); Spears discusses the earlier operas at length (262-89), and *The Bassarids* in the Auden issue of *Shenandoah*, XVIII (Winter, 1967) 85-95. *Delia or a Masque of Night* appeared in *Botteghe Oscure*, XII (1953), 164-210.

2. *Tennyson: An Introduction and a Selection by W. H. Auden* (London, 1946), p. xv. *Cf.* Isherwood's report on Auden's smoking, p. 30 above.

Selected Bibliography

(in chronological order)

1. *Books* (with abbreviations used in the text)

Poems. Oxford, 1928. Printed privately by Stephen
Spender.   *1928*

Poems. London: Faber and Faber, 1930.   *1930*

The Orators. London: Faber and Faber, 1932. (Revised
edition, 1966.)

The Dance of Death. London: Faber and Faber, 1933.

Poems. Second Edition. London: Faber and Faber, 1933.   *1933*

Poems. New York: Random House, 1934. Includes *The
Orators* and *The Dance of Death.*

The Dog Beneath the Skin (with Christopher Isherwood). New York: Random House, 1935. For convenience I quote from the London Faber and Faber
edition of 1935.   *Dog*

The Ascent of F6 (with Isherwood). New York: Random
House, 1937. For convenience I quote from the London Faber and Faber edition of 1936.   *F6*

On This Island. New York: Random House, 1937. (British
edition: *Look, Stranger!* London: Faber and Faber,
1936).   *OTI*

Letters from Iceland (with Louis MacNeice). New York:
Random House, 1937.

Spain. London: Faber and Faber, 1937.

On the Frontier (with Isherwood). New York: Random
House, 1938. For convenience I quote from the 1938
Faber and Faber edition.

Journey to a War (with Isherwood). New York: Random
House, 1939.

Another Time. New York: Random House, 1940.   *AT*

The Double Man. New York: Random House, 1941.
(Issued in London by Faber and Faber, 1941, as *New
Year Letter*).   *DM*

For the Time Being (including *The Sea and the Mirror*).
London: Faber and Faber, 1944.

The Collected Poetry of W. H. Auden. New York:

Random House, 1945.   *CP*
The Age of Anxiety. New York: Random House, 1947.
Collected Shorter Poems, 1930-1944. London: Faber and
   Faber, 1950.
The Enchafèd Flood. New York: Random House, 1950.
The Rake's Progress (with Chester Kallman). London:
   Boosey and Hawkes, 1951.
Nones. New York: Random House, 1951.
The Shield of Achilles. New York: Random House, 1955.   *Shield*
Selected Poetry. New York: Random House, 1959.
Homage to Clio. New York: Random House, 1960.   *Clio*
Elegy for Young Lovers (with Kallman). Mainz: B.
   Schott's Söhne, 1961.
The Dyer's Hand. New York: Random House, 1962.   *DH*
About the House. New York: Random House, 1965.   *House*
The Bassarids (with Kallman). Mainz: B. Schott's Söhne,
   1966.
Collected Shorter Poems, 1927-1957. London: Faber and
   Faber, 1966.

2. *Translations*

Bertolt Brecht and Kurt Weill, *The Seven Deadly Sins* (with
   Kallman). *Tulane Drama Review,* VI (Autumn 1961), 123-29.
Mozart's *The Magic Flute* (with Kallman). New York: Random
   House, 1956.
Mozart's *Don Giovanni* (with Kallman). New York: G. Schirmer,
   1961.
Goethe's *Italian Journey* (with Elizabeth Mayer). New York:
   Pantheon, 1962.
Dag Hammarskjöld, *Markings* (with Leif Sjöberg). New York:
   Knopf, 1964.

3. *Books Edited*

The Poet's Tongue: An Anthology (with John Garrett). 2 vols.
   London: G. Bell & Sons, 1935. An original selection of poetry
   for schoolboys, with a sensible introduction.
The Oxford Book of Light Verse. Oxford: Clarendon Press, 1938.
   Shows a wide acquaintance with light verse, and the introduction is an important discussion of the nature, value, and history
   of English light verse.
A Selection of the Poems of Alfred Lord Tennyson. New York:
   Doubleday, 1944. Auden sees Tennyson as "the great English
   poet of the Nursery" and explores surprising parallels between
   his work and Baudelaire's.

Selected Bibliography

Yale Series of Younger Poets, 1947-58. Perceptive introductions to the verse of new young poets.

The Portable Greek Reader. New York: Viking, 1948. Contains a valuable analysis of Greek ideals and attitudes.

Poets of the English Language (with Norman Holmes Pearson). 5 vols. New York: Viking, 1950. The introductions, all by Auden, show us his mature view of English poetry and of the philosophical, social, and formal currents that have helped to shape it.

The Living Thoughts of Kierkegaard. New York: David McKay, 1952. The introduction summarizes what Auden takes to be central in Kierkegaard's work.

The Criterion Book of Modern American Verse. New York: Criterion Books, 1956. (British edition: *The Faber Book . . .* etc. London: Faber and Faber, 1956.) A key to Auden's taste. The introduction is included in *DH.*

The Viking Book of Aphorisms (with Louis Kronenberger). New York: Viking, 1962. (British edition: *The Faber Book of Aphorisms.* London: Faber and Faber, 1964.) Splendid and original collection, with a brief introduction.

4. Contributions to Books

"Psychology and Art." *The Arts To-day,* ed. Geoffrey Grigson. London: John Lane, 1935. An apparently hasty but useful summary of the significance for art of psychology, i.e., of the "attitude to life and living relationships" best represented by Freud.

"Mimesis and Allegory." *English Institute Annual,* 1940, ed. Rudolf Kirk. New York: Columbia University Press, 1941. An important, wide-ranging essay in which, with special reference to Wagner, Auden discusses the connections between art and life, art and beliefs.

"Criticism in a Mass Society." *The Intent of the Critic,* ed. Donald A. Stauffer. Princeton: Princeton University Press, 1941. An extended discussion, pontifical but illuminating, of the problem of belief in art and of the responsibilities of critic and artist in a social democracy.

"K's Quest." *The Kafka Problem,* ed. Angel Flores. New York: New Directions, 1946. Analysis of the elements of different types of quest narratives, from the fairy tale to Kafka's kind. Only a bit of it appears in *DH.*

Untitled essay in *Modern Canterbury Pilgrims,* ed. James A. Pike. London: A. R. Mowbray, 1956. A revealing examination of Auden's personal religious history.

5. *Articles and Reviews in Periodicals* (see also those cited in the Notes to Chapter 10)

"A Literary Transference," *Southern Review*, VI (Summer, 1940), 78-86. "I cannot write objectively about Thomas Hardy because I was once in love with him." Describes Auden's youthful infatuation with Hardy's poetry and the permanent marks it left on his own work.

"A Preface to Kierkegaard," *New Republic*, CX (May 15, 1944), 683-86. Important summary of Kierkegaardian existentialism: "what he would teach is an approach to oneself, not a conclusion, a style of questioning to apply to all one's experience . . ."

"Augustus to Augustine," *New Republic*, CXI (Sept. 25, 1944), 373-76. Discusses ideas important to Auden's later poetry.

"The Dyer's Hand," *Listener*, LIII (June 16, 23, 30, 1955), 1063-66, 1109-13, 1151-54. Significant observations on the poet, the poetic process, and the special problems that face today's poet.

"On W. H. Auden's 'A Change of Air'," by George P. Elliott, Karl Shapiro, Stephen Spender, and Auden, in *The Contemporary Poet As Artist and Critic*, ed. Anthony Ostroff. Boston: Little, Brown, 1964. [First appeared in *Kenyon Review*, XXVI (Winter, 1964), 190-208.] An amusing exchange in which, replying to exasperatingly weak criticism, Auden brilliantly explains what he is currently trying to do in his poems.

"As It Seemed to Us," *New Yorker*, XLI (April 3, 1965), 159-192. A generously autobiographical review of two other writers' autobiographies.

SECONDARY SOURCES

1. *Bibliographies*

BLOOMFIELD, B. C. *W. H. Auden: A Bibliography: The Early Years through 1955*. Charlottesville: The University Press of Virginia, 1964. Foreword by Auden. The standard bibliography of Auden's writings, it includes an admittedly incomplete list of Auden criticism.

CALLAN, EDWARD. *An Annotated Check List of the Works of W. H. Auden*. Denver: Alan Swallow, 1958. List and notes are very helpful.

2. *Critical Books*

BEACH, JOSEPH WARREN. *The Making of the Auden Canon*. Minneapolis: University of Minnesota Press. Puzzles over the quirks of Auden's collections.

Selected Bibliography

BLAIR, JOHN G. *The Poetic Art of W. H. Auden.* Princeton: Princeton University Press, 1965. A perceptive general study of Auden's poetic techniques, which are seen as consistently anti-Romantic and allegorical.

EVERETT, BARBARA. *Auden.* Edinburgh: Oliver and Boyd, 1964. (Writers and Critics Series.) A brief survey of Auden's poetry, especially sensitive on the early work.

HOGGART, RICHARD. *Auden: An Introductory Essay.* London: Chatto and Windus, 1950. An early sympathetic study, strangely organized, sometimes mistaken or misleading, but often perceptive.

———. *W. H. Auden.* London: Longmans, Green, 1957. (British Council Pamphlets, No. 93.) Desultory survey.

SCARFE, FRANCIS. *Auden and After: The Liberation of Poetry, 1930-1941.* London: George Routledge & Sons, 1942. Generally hasty and superficial in treating Auden.

———. *W. H. Auden.* Monaco: Lyrebird Press, 1949. Better than Scarfe's earlier book, most apt on Auden's existentialism, but fails to see his work in its own terms.

SPEARS, MONROE K. *The Poetry of W. H. Auden: The Disenchanted Island.* New York: Oxford University Press, 1963. The closest thing to a handbook on Auden: an invaluable source of information.

———, ed. *Auden: A Collection of Critical Essays.* Englewood Cliffs, N. J.: Prentice-Hall, 1964. (Twentieth Century Views Series.) Thirteen essays on Auden's work. (Abbreviated in my text as *Auden.*)

3. Critical Essays

BAYLEY, JOHN. *The Romantic Survival: A Study in Poetic Evolution.* London: Constable & Co., 1957. Esp. pp. 129-185. A stylish, much praised study, which, along with some good analyses and sensible judgments, seems to me full of misinformation and mistaken insights.

BLOOM, ROBERT. "W. H. Auden's Bestiary of the Human," *Virginia Quarterly Review,* XLII (Spring, 1966), 207-33. An illuminating study of Auden's animal imagery.

———. "The Humanization of Auden's Early Style," *PMLA,* LXXXIII (May, 1968), 443-54. Convincingly refutes Jarrell's 1941 claim that Auden's progress in the 1930's was in the direction of impersonality and inhumanity.

CALLAN, EDWARD. "Allegory in Auden's *The Age of Anxiety,*" *Twentieth Century Literature,* X (Jan., 1965), 155-65. An indispensable guide to this poem.

——. "Auden and Kierkegaard: The Artistic Framework of *For the Time Being*," *Christian Scholar*, XLVIII (Fall, 1965), 211-23. Analyzes the poem's structure, its thought- and image-patterns.

——. "Auden's Ironic Masquerade: Criticism as Morality Play," *University of Toronto Quarterly*, XXXV (Jan., 1966), 133-43. Shows how *The Sea and the Mirror* presents Auden's literary theory.

——. "Auden's *New Year Letter*: A New Style of Architecture," *Renascence*, XVI (Fall, 1963), 13-19. Reprinted in Spears, *Auden*, pp. 152-59. Admirable analysis of the poem's Kierkegaardian structure.

——. "The Development of W. H. Auden's Poetic Theory Since 1940," *Twentieth Century Literature*, IV (Oct., 1958), 79-91. Accurate and helpful.

ENRIGHT, D. J. "Reluctant Admiration: A Note on Auden and Rilke," *The Apothecary's Shop: Essays on Literature*. London: Secker & Warburg, 1957. Perceptive, if harsh, study of Auden's use and misuse of Rilke.

HARDY, BARBARA. "The Reticence of W. H. Auden," *Review*, No. 11-12 (1964), 54-64. Enlightening on Auden's combination of reticence and strong feeling.

JARRELL, RANDALL. "Changes of Attitude and Rhetoric in Auden's Poetry," *Southern Review*, VII (Autumn, 1941), 326-49. Witty and exhaustive analysis of the rhetorical devices used in Auden's poetry as he moved from early myth to later abstraction. A brilliant article, technically accurate and highly unsympathetic.

——. "Freud to Paul: The Stages of Auden's Ideology," *Partisan Review*, XII (Fall, 1945), 437-57. A later, more cranky, less convincing attack.

LARKIN, PHILIP. "What's Become of Wystan?" *Spectator*, July 15, 1960, pp. 104-5. From the eminence of his own assured greatness, Larkin looks down disdainfully on the ruins of one who "no longer touches our imaginations."

New Verse, No. 26-27 (Nov., 1937). ("Auden Double Number.") An early collection of essays and comments on Auden.

ORWELL, GEORGE. "Inside the Whale," *Inside the Whale and Other Essays*. London: Victor Gollancz, 1940. Some hard but just words on the politics of Auden and his group.

REPLOGLE, JUSTIN. "The Auden Group," *Wisconsin Studies in Contemporary Literature*, V (Summer, 1964), 133-50. Valuable essay on who they were and what they shared.

——. "Auden's Homage to Thalia," *Bucknell Review*, XI (March, 1963), 98-117. Admirable study of the attitudes and techniques of the later poetry, which Replogle sees as better than the early work.

Selected Bibliography

——. "Auden's Marxism," *PMLA*, LXXX (Dec., 1965), 584-95. Detailed examination of a much abused subject, Auden's Marxism in the middle and later 1930's.

——. "Auden's Religious Leap," *Wisconsin Studies in Contemporary Literature*, VII (Winter-Spring, 1966), 47-76. Discusses the Kierkegaardian thought underlying Auden's longer poems of the 1940's.

——. "The Gang Myth in Auden's Early Poetry," *Journal of English and Germanic Philology*, LXI (1962), 481-95. Extremely helpful analysis of the ideas and images that made up the myth shared by Auden and his friends.

——. "Social Philosophy in Auden's Early Poetry," *Criticism*, II (Fall, 1960), 351-61. Studies Auden's non-Marxist attitudes of the early 1930's and his gradual movement toward Marxism.

Shenandoah, XVIII (Winter, 1967). Special issue on Auden. See also the essays in Spears, ed. *Auden*.

4. Especially Illuminating Collateral Books

ISHERWOOD, CHRISTOPHER. *Lions and Shadows*. New York: New Directions, 1947. Delightful account of Isherwood's early days, including much about Auden ("Hugh Weston").

SPENDER, STEPHEN. *World Within World*. New York: Harcourt, Brace, 1951. A sensitive autobiography that throws much direct and indirect light on the young Auden.

STRAVINSKY, IGOR and ROBERT CRAFT. *Memories and Commentaries*. London: Faber and Faber, 1960. Stravinsky devotes a long section of this memoir to his collaboration with Auden on *The Rake's Progress*.

SYMONS, JULIAN. *The Thirties: A Dream Revolved*. London: The Cresset Press, 1960. Useful, if not profound, account, by one of the minor writers of the thirties, of the decade's main directions, movements, feelings, events.

UPWARD, EDWARD. *Journey to the Border*. London: The Hogarth Press, 1938. An odd novel, full of Audenesque ideas and imagery, by the "Chalmers" of Isherwood's autobiography.

WARNER, REX. *The Wild Goose Chase*. New York: Knopf, 1938. A novel, by one of Auden's friends, that develops much of the group's imagery.

Index

175

Index